WITH THE PEOPLE

Second Edition Editor
Toney C. Mulhollan

First Edition Editors
Tom and Sheila Jones

www.ipibooks.com

Jesus With the People (Second Edition)
© 2017 by Illumination Publishers and DisciplesToday.org.

All rights are reserved. No part of this book may be duplicated, copied, translated, reproduced or stored mechanically, digitally or electronically without specific, written permission of the editor and publisher.
Printed in the United States of America.
ISBN: 978-1-946800-65-7.

Unless otherwise indicated, all Scripture references are from the *Holy Bible, New International Version*, copyright 1973, 1978, 1984, 2011 by the International Bible Society. Used by permission.

Scripture taken from the New Century Version®. © 2005 by Thomas Nelson. Used by permission. All rights reserved.

Cover design and interior layout by Chris Costello and Toney Mulhollan.

Copy editors: Amy Morgan and Toney Mulhollan.

Illumination Publishers is committed to caring wisely for God's creation and uses recycled paper whenever possible.

About the editor: Toney C. Mulhollan has served as the executive editor for Illumination Publishers since 2004. He has been in Christian publishing for more than forty years. Previously he served with the magazine, Biblical Illustrator, the printing ministry of the Crossroads Church and for fifteen years with Discipleship Publications  International. He and his wife, Denise make their home in Spring, Texas.

www.ipibooks.com
6010 Pinecreek Ridge Court
Spring, Texas 77379-2513

To the dedicated group of people at
Illumination Publishers
who do so much work behind the scenes.
They don't get the
headlines, but their efforts bring
encouragement and inspiration
to people around the world.
To all of them we say,
"Thank you."

CONTENTS

Never Enough of Jesus 6
    Introduction   Tom A. Jones

1. **Humility in Action** 12
    John the Baptizer   Tom A. Jones

2. **A Grateful Son** 16
    Mary, the Mother of Jesus   Larry Wood

3. **Through the Roof** 20
    The Paralytic   David Eastman

4. **Harassed and Helpless** 24
    The Crowds   Mohan Nanjundan

5. **Going Deeper** 28
    The Samaritan Woman   Lori Bynum

6. **Blind Unbelief is Sure to Err** 32
    The Man Born Blind   Toney Mulhollan

7. **The Divine Position** 36
    The Widow of Nain   Emily Bringardner

8. **The Call of the Wild** 40
    The Gerasene Demoniac   Henry Kreite

9. **From Compliment to Confrontation** 44
    Nicodemus   John Mannel

10. **The Price is Always Higher** 48
    Three Men Called to Discipleship   Toney Mulhollan

11. **He Looked at Him and Loved Him** 52
    The Rich Young Ruler   François and Penny Faure

12. **Dinnertime Discipling** 56
    The Twelve Apostles   Toney Mulhollan

13. **God Comes Looking** 60
    The Man Blind from Birth   Nancy Mannel

14. **A Friend of Sinners** 64
    Zacchaeus   Greg and Shelley Metten

15. **The Greatest in the Kingdom** 68
    The Little Children   Al and Gloria Baird

16. **No 'Dogs' in Heaven** 72
    The Canaanite Woman   Sheila Jones

CONTENTS

17. **A Crowd-Pleaser** 76
    The Bleeding Woman and Jairus' Daughter   *Karen Louis*

18. **Seeing and Not Seeing** 80
    Simon the Pharisee and the Sinful Woman   *Diane Brown*

19. **Give or Take?** 84
    Matthew, the Tax Collector   *John Bringardner*

20. **Perceiving Potential** 88
    The Apostle Peter   *Brian Homet*

21. **The Disciple Whom Jesus Loved** 92
    The Apostle John   *Steve Brown*

22. **Selection and Delegation** 96
    The Seventy-Two   *Andrew Fleming*

23. **Hard Heads, Hard Hearts** 100
    The Pharisees   *Brian Felushko*

24. **A Real Friend** 104
    Martha and Mary   *Tricia Staten*

25. **Death Be Not Proud** 108
    Lazarus   *G. Steve Kinnard*

26. **Entrusted and Transformed** 112
    Mary Magdalene   *Caryn Homet*

27. **Giving All She Had** 116
    The Widow at the Temple   *Pat Gempel*

28. **Political 'Principle'** 120
    Pontius Pilate   *Steve Staten*

29. **Love Thy Enemy** 124
    Judas Iscariot   *Tammy Fleming*

30. **Eyes Opened to Faith** 128
    Disciples on the Road to Emmaus   *Jeanie Shaw*

31. **From Doubt to Faith** 132
    The Apostle Thomas   *Curt Simmons*

    Still with the People 136
    Epilogue   *Tom A. Jones*

    The Enduring Impact of Jesus 138
    Appendix   *Toney Mulhollan*

Never Enough of Jesus
Introduction

Did you ever look at the person who's been your friend for years and think, *Do I know this person, really?* Maybe it's your spouse. Maybe it's your best friend. Doesn't it amaze you when they say or do something you completely do not expect? It may be a bit like hitting an unexpected speed bump, but it also opens up whole new worlds of possibility in your relationship.

In every generation—no, in every year in the life of every disciple—there is the need to rediscover Jesus. In the history of civilization, there has been no one like him, but time and tradition have a way of dulling our understanding of him. We can speak of him often, but who he really is and the ways he interacted with people can become foggy in our minds.

I cannot remember the first time I ever heard his name. I know it was when I was a small child. But this much I do know: The Jesus I discovered later as a college student bore almost no resemblance to the Jesus I had known before. The Jesus of my early years was a Jesus of southern American culture and my family's traditions. The Jesus I discovered as I entered my twenties was the Jesus of Scripture, and remarkably, there was little relationship between the two. From that experience I learned an important lesson: We can think we know Jesus, when we actually have so much more we need to learn. There will *always* be the need for fresh readings of the gospels and fresh efforts to look more deeply into the kind of man Jesus was, what motivated him and how he loved people.

My guess is that most who will read this book will have been "taught about Jesus accurately" (like Apollos in Acts 18:25), but these things are being written with the conviction that we all, like Apollos, have so much more to understand. Well into the ministry of Jesus, Peter learned that we can think we have arrived in our understanding when, in fact, we really don't get it at all. (See Matthew 16:13-23). He boldly confessed Jesus to be the Christ, received affirmation for his confession, and then promptly got a shocking rebuke when he made it clear that he totally misunderstood what Jesus was all about. If a man who had walked daily with Jesus for months and was destined to become the first leader in God's first-century movement could be so wrong, how could we ever be so sure we have arrived—whoever "we" may be and whatever our history and spiritual pedigree?

The test of any movement of God is how continually it seeks to rediscover Jesus and how determined it is never to set up a monument to its present understandings. Listen to how Paul describes Jesus:

> My purpose is that they may be encouraged in heart and united in love, so that they may have the full riches of complete understanding, in order that they may know the mystery of God, namely, *Christ, in whom are hidden all the treasures of wisdom and knowledge* (Colossians 2:2-3, emphasis added).

With *all* the treasures of wisdom and knowledge being found in Jesus, we can all grow in our understanding of him. He is an endless source of new insights and new perspectives on life, good and evil, love, spirituality and the human heart.

Jesus with the People

Because we find such a richness of life in Jesus, we could seek a greater understanding of him in countless ways. In this book, we are taking advantage of just one of those. We have selected thirty-one people or, in some cases, groups of people whom Jesus met and taught and loved. We have asked each contributor to this volume to spend time getting into the skin of their person (or persons) and into the heart of Jesus, as it is revealed in his interaction with them. From these personal encounters Jesus had with people, we can gain a wealth of knowledge about the nature of God and about the way we need to relate to the people around us. We will see more clearly what our purpose in this life is and how we can fulfill it.

Several years ago my friend Sam Laing introduced me to a book written about Jesus over 100 years ago and long since out of print. *Jesus the Same* by Charles Edward Jefferson contains some powerful descriptions of this man we seek to understand. Early in his book, Jefferson writes:

> When we open our New Testament, we find a man looking at us, who although not a professional revolutionist has been the cause of many revolutions, and who although not a disturber of the peace has repeatedly turned the world upside down.... He dares to reverse all human standards, confounds the wise by things which are foolish and confounds things which are mighty by the things which are weak. He has much to say about authority and power, and it is his claim that he can make all things new.... If his ideas have in them the force of dynamite, and if his personality has power to change the policy of empires and even the temper of the human heart, it may be that this man is the very man the modern world is looking for in its wild quest for a way of deliverance from its miseries and woes.

Then Jefferson adds words that support the approach we are taking in this book:

> When we study [Jesus'] method, we discover that his supreme concern is for the rightness of heart of the *individual man*. This molder of empires gives himself to the task of molding individual men. This arch revolutionist starts his conflagrations in the *individual soul*. He draws one man to him, infuses into him a new spirit, sends him after one brother man, who in time goes after a third man, and this third man after a fourth, and thus does he weld a chain by means of which Caesar shall be dragged from his throne. Strange as it may seem, he has nothing to say about heredity, and stranger still nothing to say about environment. He keeps his eyes upon the soul, and by changing this he alters the environment and also the

currents of the blood down through many generations (emphasis added).

    Jesus preached to the multitudes, but we get to know him best as we see him face to face with individual people. He shows them, in an up-close and personal way, how God feels about them and what God calls them to be. Just the fact that there are so many stories of the Son of God interacting with individuals tells us much about the character of God, but when we look more closely at those stories, even more truths are revealed. Every encounter he had, whether with a nameless sinful woman or with a well-known Jewish leader, is a window into the soul of Jesus.

    Do you want to know Jesus better? Do you hunger and thirst for more of his character and heart? Do you recognize that no matter where you are on your spiritual journey, there is more about Jesus that you *don't* know than what you *do* know?

    Our prayer is that in the next month or so you will find yourself listening to Jesus, watching him carefully, wrestling with his words and feeling his pulse like never before. In this book we will not come close to fulfilling your need to learn of him, but prayerfully, we can take you further in his direction than you have been. If we succeed, you will have truth that you very much need, but also a continuing thirst for more. We can never get enough of Jesus!

—Tom A. Jones

JESUS WENT THROUGH ALL
THE TOWNS AND VILLAGES,
TEACHING IN THEIR SYNAGOGUES,
PREACHING THE GOOD NEWS
OF THE KINGDOM
AND HEALING EVERY
DISEASE AND SICKNESS.

Matthew 9:35

•1•
Humility in Action
John the Baptizer

TOM A. JONES
Hermitage, Tennessee

> Then Jesus came from Galilee to the Jordan to be baptized by John. But John tried to deter him, saying, "I need to be baptized by you, and do you come to me?"
> Jesus replied, "Let it be so now; it is proper for us to do this to fulfill all righteousness." Then John consented.
> Matthew 3:13-15

If you judge according to style, John the Baptizer and Jesus of Nazareth were hardly two peas in a pod. One did his preaching out in the desert; the other worked mostly in the villages and cities. One lived a Spartan lifestyle and was the first-century equivalent of the earthy-crunchy soul; the other, while no candidate for the country club, did have a reputation for showing up where there was plenty of food and drink (and even on occasion for providing the wine).

Humility Times Two

With the attention of the crowds focused on him and with incredible personal power within his grasp, John followed God's plan, instead of a human one, and humbled himself. "After me will come one who is more powerful than I, whose sandals I am not fit to carry" (Matthew 3:11b). With Jesus not yet on the scene, John called people to focus not on him, but on the one coming later. Humility in action.

But then here comes Jesus, and what is his first move with John? "Then Jesus came from Galilee to be baptized by John" (3:13). Jesus comes out, most likely standing in line with all the others, with the desire to place his body in John's hands for immersion. Humility in action.

Then John responds. "But John tried to deter him, saying, 'I need to be baptized by you, and do you come to me?'" (3:13-14). Jesus, in so many words, says "This is the right thing. I need to humble myself and submit to your baptism" (3:15a). In humility, John then submitted to Jesus' submission (3:15b). Surely, Satan hated it. These two powerful men just kept humbling themselves before one another, and the bond of unity grew tighter and tighter.

Such a pattern continued throughout their lives. As their ministries overlapped, there was the inevitable tendency of some to try to pit the two against each other. Some of John's disciples complained that Jesus was baptizing and that everyone was going to him (John 3:25-26). "To this John replied, 'A man can receive only what is given him from heaven. You yourselves can testify that I said, "I am not the Christ but am sent ahead of him." ...He must become greater; I must become less'" (John 3:27-30). John did not grasp and grab for what was his. He stayed humble.

Staying Humble

But then, when the word spread among the Pharisees that Jesus, or at least his disciples, were gaining and baptizing more disciples than John (John 4:1), Jesus left his Judean ministry and went back to Galilee, deliberately avoiding a situation where he and John could be depicted as rivals. The Jesus who did not grasp his equality with God (Philippians 2:6), did not grasp his ministry either. He stayed humble. Spiritual leaders around the world, are you paying attention?

Later when John was battling with Satan in the loneliness of prison and had some doubts about Jesus (John was a man like us), he sent some disciples to ask Jesus an important question. Jesus gave John's messengers the needed answer and then broke into a speech about the greatness of John, culminating with these words: "I tell you the truth: Among those born of women there has not risen anyone greater than John the Baptist..." (Matthew 11:11). If we are looking for a prototype of unity, we need go no further than Jesus and John the Baptist. It was humility that kept them bonded together, even when Satan was working to divide.

Is your conviction growing as deep as mine? There is only one thing that keeps people from being united: pride. There is one thing that will bring them together: humility. Whenever there is division, you can smell a rat and the rat's name is "Pride." Every time there is division, you can be absolutely sure he is there.

When unity does not exist among believers, you can be sure of this: People are not willing to pay the price. Their pride means too much to them. They are too proud of their ideas, their position, their reputation, their following, their publication, their agenda, their book, their emphasis, their dream, or maybe even *their* plan for unity. They grasp and hold to what is theirs. And Satan says, "Maybe I couldn't get Jesus and John, but I've got these yokels right where I want them." That bothers me! It bothers me enough to change. And so I pray, "God, crush me whenever you need to. Bring me as low as I need to go. Take away all my stinkin' pride! Get every lousy attitude out of my heart that keeps me from being absolutely one with others who want your message to go around the world."

"He who humbles himself will be exalted." Jesus' relationship with John is a model for all leaders. It is a model for every marriage. It is a model for *every* relationship in the kingdom of God. In Jesus of Nazareth we learn that God is humble and that he honors all who humble themselves.

LIFE APPLICATION

1. When are times in your life when you feel a sense of rivalry? How about in your marriage? What about in relationship to your parents? How about in the workplace? What about in the church?

2. If you were to imitate John and Jesus, what changes would you make immediately?

3. Do you have a deep and burning conviction that there is no quality in this world more important than humility? Do you have an equally deep conviction that God blesses and honors humility?

4. What relationship do you have that would be greatly changed by a good talk about how you want to show humility and not pride?

· 2 ·
A Grateful Son
Mary, the Mother of Jesus

LARRY WOOD
Durham, North Carolina

Read Luke 2:25-35, John 19:25-17

> *Beside our Lord on Calvary*
> > *Behold His mother near;*
> *Her love so true, so strong, so pure*
> > *Has conquered all her fear.*
>
> *She dares the fury of His foes,*
> > *Endures the scoffer's scorn,*
> *That she might share the Savior's woes*
> > *And comfort Him forlorn.*
>
> *O come, behold you mothers all*
> > *Of every race and state;*
> *Behold in her the pattern true*
> > *For you to emulate.*
>
> *And come you sons, behold the Christ,*
> > *The noblest son of earth!*
> *In death's dark hour He looks in love*
> > *On her who gave Him birth.*
>
> *Come Holy Spirit, breathe on us,*
> > *His love to each impart;*
> *Regenerate the soul, create*
> > *His image in our heart.*
> > > Anonymous

A baby nursing. An infant taking his first steps. A toddler playing. A small child growing and developing into a teenager. Finally, the child maturing into an adult. All of these, and so many more are the memories of a mother.

Now imagine the tragedy of a woman who outlives her child. A woman whose final memory of her child is his burial. A woman who must endure the pain of having the life she nurtured from birth end abruptly. It has been said that there is no greater pain than that of a parent who must bury a child and live with that memory.

Yet, as John records Jesus' crucifixion, he alone notes Jesus' final words to Mary. As the torture of the cross is coming to an agonizing end and Jesus is on the verge of giving up his spirit, he stops the process of redeeming humanity to focus for one final moment on his mother. "Dear woman, here is your son," he says. Then he turns to one of his best friends, the disciple John, saying, "Here is your mother." All our excuses for neglecting our families die with Jesus, as he spends his last moments thinking of his mother and providing for her. Later as Mary reflected on what a blessing it was to be the mother of Jesus Christ, I am sure her mind often replayed this his final act of honor and loyalty.

God *Was* One of Us

Jesus was a normal child. He related to Mary as any child would relate to his mother. As a Jewish boy, he learned at her feet. As an adolescent, he was marked by awkwardness and immaturity that typifies young boys. As a young man, he was apprenticed in the family business of carpentry. In every way, Jesus submitted himself to being a normal human. As a normal child, Jesus learned well the lesson to honor your mother (Exodus 20:12). While he would never have advocated the worship of Mary, what Jesus did at the cross exemplifies how Jesus held his mother in the highest esteem.

The gospels detail quite specifically account after account of Jesus' life. Yet, the gospel writers, led by the Spirit of God, give only glimpses into Jesus' childhood and his formative years. Why? It seems likely the answer lies in the fact that Jesus first had to embrace all humanness. He had diapers changed; he learned to walk, to talk and to play. Unlike most gods of Greek mythology who came on the scene as fully mature adults, Jesus submitted himself to being a child as the first step in his commitment to being fully human. This fact begins and defines Jesus' relationship with Mary. She was the mother God had chosen for his only son Jesus. She was the one God had chosen to nurture and facilitate Jesus' growth in wisdom and in stature (Luke 2:52). Mary, a virgin pledged to be married, most likely a teenager, would be the mother to God's son.

Boy Wonder?

Was Jesus a supernatural child, as some of the non-canonical gospels suggest? Or was he a normal boy? A toddler who asked those charming questions that only toddlers ask? Surely, he had sniffles like any other child and needed his knee bandaged and cleaned like any other child. Mary's and the Gospels' silence answer this question ever so loudly. Jesus' childhood was that of any other Jewish boy, and Mary was his mother in every sense of the word. Jesus knew the ridicule his mother endured for him. He knew the prophecy of Simeon that a sword would pierce Mary's soul one day. Obviously, Jesus comprehended the sacrifice of God, his Father, but it is equally true that Jesus understood and appreciated the sacrifices Mary made for him as his mother.

Four times in the gospels we see Jesus relate to Mary directly. Each incident reveals how deeply Jesus honored her. He obeyed her (Luke 2:51). According to some interpretations, he allowed her to influence him when he performed his first miracle (John 2:1-11). However, while he was intensely loyal, he did not allow his devotion to Mary make him sentimental (Mark 3:20-21, 31-35). In the end, he protected and provided for her needs as he died on a cross.

Never Too Busy to Call

Jesus, our God who became man, was not so "spiritual" that he neglected and dismissed the needs of others, especially the mother who gave him birth—not even at the cross. What a challenge to busy disciples who often neglect the needs of our immediate families. Husbands, are we too busy to honor ours wives by listening to them? Mothers and fathers, are we too busy to invest in our relationships with our children? Are we as children too busy with the urgencies of our lives to spend time with our parents?

Few of us would confess such neglect. But our guilt is revealed by our schedule books. The fact is that many of us spend more time relating to strangers than we do in building the relationships closest to us. As Paul told Timothy, a busy evangelist, we deny our faith when we neglect to provide for our relatives (1 Timothy 5:7-8).

Jesus eventually won the soul of the person who knew him better than any other—not by a loud voice, not with profound logic, not with fire, zeal or fervency. Jesus won Mary's soul with a relationship! Jesus became Mary's Messiah because he knew just how to relate to her. And, as a child to his mother, he gave her the honor she deserved. Sound too simple? That was and remains Jesus' way!

LIFE APPLICATION

1. How is your relationship with your parents? Could it be held out as an example of how to win a family member to Jesus?

2. Are you so busy with your ministry, career or life that you end up neglecting those closest to you, especially your parents? What changes do you need to make to provide for the emotional and spiritual needs of your family?

3. Have you allowed sentimental feelings for family keep you from doing the will of God? Why do such decisions not really show honor to your family?

4. What kind of memories are you making with your current family? Your roommate? Your spouse? Your children? Your parents?

·3·
Through the Roof
The Paralytic

DAVID EASTMAN
Indianapolis, Indiana

Since they could not get him to Jesus because of the crowd, they made an opening in the roof above Jesus and, after digging through it, lowered the mat the paralyzed man was lying on. When Jesus saw their faith, he said to the paralytic, "Son, your sins are forgiven."
Mark 2:4-5

The afternoon sun set on the hot Palestinian day, easing the discomfort of the four men and their burden. They wound their way through the narrow streets to the boisterous crowd crushed into a modest home in the center of Capernaum. The atmosphere was electric, the mob shoving, pushing, crowding to get a better view of—or, if nothing else, a better listen to—the man who was the center of attention. He was nondescript: not tall, not short. Yet, all eyes and ears were riveted on him.

The four men with their cargo tried vainly to move through the crowd, but were rudely turned away. Finally, the "cargo," a paralyzed man lying on a litter between them, whispered to the four men and pointed to the rear of the structure. "We can't do that," began one, but was silenced by the pleading stare of the paralytic. Straining and grunting, the men carried their friend up the back staircase onto the thatched roof. After setting him down, one ran to retrieve four pieces of wound hemp and a small pickax.

Down below, in the central room of the small dwelling, pieces of mud and thatch began to fall from the ceiling in front of the teacher, raining on the heads of those who sat in the choicest spots. The teacher paused in his discourse and glanced upward.

Suddenly, a bright shaft of sunlight angled into the room and was abruptly cut off as a dirty woolen blanket tied on all four corners was carefully lowered through the opening and came to rest four feet above the ground, swaying back and forth before the smiling eyes of the teacher. "Jesus," the paralyzed man said with a glint in his eye, "it's great to have you back in Capernaum!"
Jesus replied with a smile, "Son, your sins are forgiven."

If you had been in the throng crowded around Jesus, how would you have felt about the audacity of these five men? If you were Peter and Andrew (who may have owned the house with the newly damaged roof), how would you have responded? How different was the response of Jesus! Always the Master, Jesus demonstrates his love for people in the way he deals with the crowds, the unbelieving religious and the faithful five.

Jesus with the Crowds

Everywhere he went, Jesus drew a crowd (cf. Matthew 8:1, 11:7, 12:46, 13:34, 14:14, 15:10, 15:29-30, 20:29, 21:8, to name a few). He spoke with authority—with conviction—because he deeply cared about people, and they loved it. What Jesus preached to them was the Word—no watered down philosophy there! (Mark 2:2). Over twenty years ago, I came to church as a completely irreligious skeptic. No one tried to philosophize with me; rather, a man powerfully preached the Word and laid bare the inner workings of my sinful heart. That's what gave me hope that things in my life could be different, permanently!

Our obvious challenge from the example of Jesus is that we need to care enough to gather a crowd! People need to constantly be our focus: They need to be in our homes, in our Saturday plans, the focus of our lunch hour. If we are picky and selective, if we just reach out to people with whom we are comfortable, then we will be minimally effective. Our friends Willie and Tonya Flores, were ministry leaders in Los Angeles, were a constant model of this. Their home was continually filled with people: dinner guests, parties, open houses and people studying the Bible. It was no wonder that they were consistently helping people become disciples of Jesus.

Jesus with the Religious

Of all the varied personalities Jesus interacted with, the religious ones irritated him the most. Their slavery to legalistic minutiae angered him (Matthew 23:23-24); their stubborn hearts distressed him (Mark 3:1-5); and their narrow-minded legalism ultimately prompted his most stinging rebukes (see all of Matthew 23). Yet, it was absolutely a desire of Jesus' heart to save these religious people. In the account of the paralytic in Mark 2, we see Jesus' heart as he responds to the accusations of the teachers of the law who were there—not the caustic heart of a man determined to "put these men in their place," but a compassionate heart desperate to help them see the truth. He reveals in words the secrets of their hearts (Mark 2:8), and then, by his miraculous healing gives them everything they need to believe and receive true freedom!

I think of Robert and Julie (not their real names), two who, when they were met by disciples, had previously "prayed Jesus into their hearts" in the way so common in many churches. They were religious, but completely powerless—they were not seeing God work in their lives as they read about him in the Scriptures. They needed people in their lives who were willing to love them, to spend time with them, to patiently model the lifestyle of genuine discipleship. Within a few months they were won over, baptized into Christ, and are now living productive, powerful spiritual lives. This story could be repeated many times over if we were willing to invest our hearts in helping people as Jesus did.

Jesus with the Faithful

Jesus gets the greatest joy from interacting with people who believe. We see it here. We see it with the centurion (Luke 7:9). When Jesus returns the second time, what he will be looking for is faith (Luke 18:8).

What fires Jesus up? He looks for faith! He saw it in these fellows who made their presumptuous entrance through the roof. Why did they come to Jesus like no one else ever had? Because they absolutely *believed* that Jesus had the power to heal! Jesus gets excited about those who are willing to believe in his ability to change the spiritual destination of people!

Clearly this story shows us that Jesus was most tolerant of any interruption that came because of faith. If we follow Jesus, the smallest seed of faith that we see in others should encourage and excite us. We should be eager to nurture it and help it grow into a great plant.

LIFE APPLICATION

1. How big is your crowd? Do you have names, numbers and birthdays of your non-Christian friends that you refer to daily?

2. How do you *feel* about religious people? Do they engender disgust or compassion? Are you eager to imitate Matthew 23 before patiently "explaining to them the way of God more adequately"? (Acts 18:26).

3. Do you "see" the faith of others? Does it make you happy, or do you struggle with jealousy toward those who have more?

4. At least two things amaze Jesus. One is faith, and the other a lack of it (cf. Matthew 8:10, Mark 6:6). The five men in Mark 2 pleased Jesus—is he pleased when he sees your faith, or amazed by your lack of it?

5. Evaluate your life in light of this statement of Paul: "The only thing that counts is faith expressing itself through love" (Galatians 5:6b). In the past week, how have you lived that verse out in your own life? How can you do it better this week?

.4.
Harassed and Helpless
The Crowds

MOHAN NANJUNDAN
London, England

When he saw the crowds, he had compassion on them, because they were harassed and helpless like sheep without a shepherd.

Matthew 9:36

"He had compassion on them." In my work with HOPE Worldwide, I recently went with some of the New Delhi staff members of HOPE to visit the Village of Hope Leprosy Colony opened in 1994. We met with our architects to review the progress being made on the final phase of construction. We also talked with the leprosy patients already living there to address any problems they might be facing.

That morning, two patients, both leaders among their people, were extremely unhappy. One was unhappy about the progress of repairs in his section of the village while the other disagreed with the architects' choice of roofing materials in his area.

As we discussed the problems, it became apparent that my two friends were not going to budge from their positions. I felt my blood begin to boil. I thought to myself, *These guys have just moved from mud huts to real houses for free, and suddenly they've become experts with attitudes!* Looking back, I know that my conversation with them wasn't very godly.

How different I was from Jesus! He dealt with the masses all the time. They weren't always grateful. They often had grievances and were rarely polite. Yet, Jesus had compassion on them.

He Saw the Need, Not the Negatives

Jesus was always able to look beyond people's outward behavior to the need within. That's why he saw them as harassed and helpless. How does a person who is harassed and helpless behave? Probably with some irritation, like the two leprosy patients. Probably a little mistrusting. It's hard to trust when you've been on the raw end of a deal all your life.

But still, Jesus saw the need. He saw beyond the paralytic's physical condition to his true need for forgiveness (Mark 2:5). He saw the invalid's need for hope at the poolside (John 5:6).

That morning at the Village of Hope, I was being selfish. The people needed patience. They got anger. They needed a shepherd, and instead they got a "sheep shearer" ready to "cut them down to size." In case you are wondering, I've repented! I had to if I wanted to keep following Jesus.

He Saw the Potential, Not the Problems

Immediately after our theme verse in Matthew 9, Jesus said to his disciples, "The harvest is plentiful...."

When I see a crowd that is harassed and helpless, I think, *Problems, problems, problems.* When Jesus saw a crowd he thought, *Harvest, harvest, harvest.* I would not be surprised if many faithful disciples were telling Jesus that it was wiser to evangelize in the "suburbs," where there were less "problem" people, but Jesus would not be swayed.

Jesus always saw the potential in people, not the problems. That's why he inspired such incredible change in those around him. Frequently, we lose vision for people because we see their problems while failing to see their potential. Fruitlessness, fallaways and failures add to our pessimism, especially with our families and those closest to us.

I was convicted when the parents of Raghu Katragadda, an evangelist in New Delhi, became Christians. I had watched Raghu reach out to them over the years, very persistently. I appreciated his faith, but always felt it would take a very long time for them to change. His parents reminded me of my own parents: well-educated, respectable, upper-class Hindus who did not readily see their need for the gospel of Jesus. His father had a great government job, and his mother was a university professor. Raghu reached out to them for six years. Bit by bit, he chiseled away their doubts and challenged their convictions. He never lost sight of their potential to be great disciples, and he just ignored the problems. In November 1994 they were baptized into Christ!

To lose our vision for people is to lose sight of God's ability to change hearts. Our attitude should always be, "If Jesus could change me, then he can change anyone."

He Made a Response, Not a Retreat

The people needed a shepherd. Jesus responded; he became their shepherd. In addition to this, he raised up other shepherds (Matthew 9:38-10:4).

I once heard a lesson in which the preacher said, "Compassion is passion that leads to action." To simply feel bad for someone is not Christlike compassion. Jesus felt compassion on the crowds, then acted immediately!

How often have we seen a need or gotten convicted in a message, but then not acted? Sometimes we feel bad and pray, but still don't act. There are times when all we can *do* is pray, but most of the time we need to pray and then do something. Jesus taught his disciples to pray for workers (Matthew 9:38) and then to go and be workers! (Matthew 10:1). I wonder how many times things don't get done because Christians fail to realize that they are the answers to their own prayers. "If it is to be, it is up to me," should always be our motto.

I appreciate the HOPE Worldwide Youth Corps. These teenage disciples who have served in Manila, Johannesburg, Mexico City, Abidjan and other cities with great problems, have seen the need and have responded. They've ignored the negative and have not retreated from the harassed and helpless crowds.

The challenge for us, as imitators of Christ, is to respond to, not retreat from, the needs around us. We must be active in helping the poor and meeting physical needs, but more importantly we must be determined to see and meet the spiritual needs of the masses. Like Jesus, we must stay focused and committed in order to seek and save what is lost.

Often the people we meet are not that lovable—they may be selfish, obnoxious, demanding or loaded down with problems. But Jesus looks at them and has compassion on them. Do we?

LIFE APPLICATION

1. At your workplace, home or school, are you meeting needs, or do you always find yourself reacting to the way people treat you? Make a list of the needs you see where you are—physical, emotional and spiritual. Pray about them daily and make a plan to meet those needs.

2. Is your ministry group involved in helping the poor in your area? If not, talk to your leaders this week about getting involved.

3. Have you lost your vision for change in people? If you have given up on anyone, repent today and boldly share your faith again.

·5·
Going Deeper
The Samaritan Woman

LORI BYNUM
Ft. Walton Beach, Florida

Read John 4

> Many of the Samaritans from that town believed in him, because of the woman's testimony, "He told me everything I ever did."
>
> John 4:39

"If only you really knew me..." How many of us have said these words to ourselves? We want to be known, but we keep a safe distance. We want to be loved, but we fight being real. We want acceptance, but we fear the openness that may bring condemnation. We play our cards close to our chest, and we don't let anyone get too close. Then along comes Jesus. A man with X-ray vision that sees right through to the very depths of our hearts. He not only sees who we are inside, but he helps us to see ourselves.

Getting Spiritual

The person in our story was a woman from Samaria. She was minding her own business, but she ran into Jesus and was never the same. She was only going about her chores, drawing water from the well, but she came face to face with a man who would change her life forever.

Jesus was tired, hungry and thirsty as he sat down by the well. He could have been preoccupied with his own needs, but instead he saw hers. "Will you give me a drink?" he asked. The woman was amazed. She could hear by his accent that he was a Jew. Jewish men would not even address their own wives publicly. Everyone knew Jews hated Samaritans. They would rather walk around Samaria, than walk through it—even if it meant traveling farther. And Samaritan women were considered much worse. The fact that he spoke to her told her in an instant that there was something very different about this man.

Jesus initially talked to her about water from the well, but he found a way to steer the conversation in spiritual directions. "Everyone who drinks this water will be thirsty again, but whoever drinks the water I give him will never thirst. Indeed, the water I give him will become in him a spring of water welling up to eternal life" (John 4:13-14). As she heard his words, the woman was still thinking literally, but Jesus definitely had her attention.

"Go, call your husband and come back." Jesus told her. He knew the condition of her life. He knew that she had been married five times and was currently living with someone who was not her husband. He confronted her sin to help her see the emptiness of her life. He wanted her to see what she was without God. And he wanted to fulfill the deepest desire of her heart—a desire for an eternal lasting relationship with God.

Opening Her Eyes

Suddenly, due to discomfort or embarrassment, the stunned woman changed the subject. She asked a "religious question." *(Don't get too close, Jesus. Don't get too personal.)* She tried to look good and sound good. She was thirsty for acceptance and love, but she donned a religious mask to hide the void in her heart that Jesus had exposed. She feared what she needed the most. But again, Jesus skillfully drove out her fears with his love. He brought the conversation back to her life, her sin and her need for forgiveness. He held up the standard of God. He taught her God's expectations for her life—that she worship in spirit and in truth. He didn't let her superficiality make him that way; he helped her be genuine. "The purposes of a man's heart are deep waters, but a man of understanding draws them out" (Proverbs 20:5). Jesus penetrated the fortress this woman had put up to shield herself from the pain of rejection.

He opened her eyes to who he was. He showed her he was more than a prophet—he was the Messiah—the one who came to save not only the Jews, but the whole world, even her. How her heart must have raced as she went back and shared all this with the people in her town.

This woman knew Jesus was the Messiah because he told her everything she ever did (John 4:39). In my own life, this is the very thing that attracted me to Jesus and to the people who were like him. I remember reading the Bible and being amazed at how accurately it described me. I was attracted to Jesus, but afraid as well. I remember trying to keep at a distance the Christians who wanted to know me. I put up a wall to keep them from getting too close. I was nice, but superficial with them. I was afraid of being looked down on and being rejected by them because of my sins: immorality, drunkenness, selfishness and pride.

I was also afraid of seeing who I really was. It was too painful. But I remember how the disciples loved me anyway, how they confronted me with the truth about God and myself. They were not intimidated or cowardly when asking me questions about my relationship with God and other people. As I struggled with the ugliness of my own sin, I finally saw how much I needed Jesus. When I was forgiven and when I realized what I had found, I was so excited that I couldn't wait to tell others about him. I was like the Samaritan woman who ran back to share with everyone about the man who spoke the truth to her and set her free.

To set people free, we must be like Jesus. We must not relate to them in shallow ways, but instead help them to understand the truth about the Bible and the truth about themselves. When we study the Bible superficially with people, we are cowardly and we are not helping them see who they really are without God. We need to ask the difficult questions—the ones that make people feel uncomfortable. We need to expose their sin so they will see their deepest need for Jesus the Savior. Jesus doesn't want people to conform to a set of standards or beliefs, he wants to change them from the inside out.

Jesus' love and acceptance allowed the woman at the well to be real and to change. His attention made her feel special and wanted. Jesus, a man who could move the hearts of thousands, took time to reach out, convict and heal for all of eternity this often shunned Samaritan. What is he teaching you?

LIFE APPLICATION

1. Do you remember the first time you saw the truth about yourself—that you were a sinner? What was your response then, and what is your response now?

2. In what ways are you superficial with the people you are sharing Jesus with, and how can you overcome this?

3. How can you better show the love and acceptance of Jesus in your life to those around you?

·6·
Blind Unbelief is Sure to Err
The Man Born Blind

TONEY MULHOLLAN
Spring, Texas

As he went along, he saw a man blind from birth. His disciples asked him, "Rabbi,a who sinned, this man or his parents, that he was born blind?"

"Neither this man nor his parents sinned," said Jesus, "but this happened so that the works of God might be displayed in him. As long as it is day, we must do the works of him who sent me. Night is coming, when no one can work. While I am in the world, I am the light of the world."

After saying this, he spit on the ground, made some mud with the saliva, and put it on the man's eyes. "Go," he told him, "wash in the Pool of Siloam" (this word means "Sent"). So the man went and washed, and came home seeing.

His neighbors and those who had formerly seen him begging asked, "Isn't this the same man who used to sit and beg?" Some claimed that he was.

Others said, "No, he only looks like him."

But he himself insisted, "I am the man."

"How then were your eyes opened?" they asked.

He replied, "The man they call Jesus made some mud and put it on my eyes. He told me to go to Siloam and wash. So I went and washed, and then I could see."

John 9:1-11

It is easy to be blinded to the important issues of life. Many times just the hectic pace of life keeps us from growing in faith and blinds us to the ways that God can use us to change the world. John 9 gives witness to attitudes and actions that blind us from being faithful disciples of Jesus. Let's look at that chapter and study four groups of people who could see but were blind.

In John 9:1–6, Jesus' disciples meet a man who was blind from birth. They immediately question Jesus about who had sinned, this man or his parents, that he would be born blind. It was commonly accepted that any tragedy in life was directly caused by sin. Jesus quickly dispelled that notion and asserted that God had allowed this to happen so that a great work might be displayed in this blind man's life. Jesus begins this great work by spitting on the ground, making some mud and putting it on the man's eyes. He commands him to go the pool of Siloam and wash. The man obeys and immediately receives his sight.

Even the men closest to Jesus were blinded to the purposes of God. It is clear from this passage that God works from the very time that people are born to enable them to have an opportunity to hear the good news. It is amazing that some people have waited their entire lives so that one day some disciple can stop, help them and share with them about Jesus. We need to have faith to see God's hand and purpose in every situation. **When we have this kind of faith, we will not be blinded to the purposes of God.**

Soon after receiving his sight the blind man goes home and shares with his parents and neighbors this great news. His neighbors were more than shocked, and despite the blind man's claims, they doubted whether this man was their neighbor at all, speculating that he only looked like the blind man.

It is amazing that his closest neighbors and people who had seen him begging for years didn't recognize him. But perhaps we should not be surprised at this. Though having seen him for years, his neighbors had only a superficial relationship with him. Superficiality blinds us to the real needs of others. We never get below the surface and touch the heart. Superficiality will make you alone and aloof and only a surface dweller.

As disciples we must ask ourselves: How well do we know our neighbors? Have we served them, had them into our home for a meal or for a party? How well do you know your workmates, those people you see every day? How about your relatives; have you reached out to them, loved and encouraged them? The only way we can reach our neighbors, family and friends is to get below the surface and build genuine friendships. It has been said often, and I have found it to be true: The only people we really convert are the ones we make our friends. **This interaction between the blind man and his neighbors demonstrates that Jesus needs disciples who are not blinded by superficiality.**

The next people to consider in this eye-opening story are the parents of the blind man. John 9:18–23 records their reaction to their son's healing. It is apparent from this passage that the parents had kept themselves aloof from their own son. Considering that any disability was looked upon as a curse from God, it is not surprising that they even allowed their son to beg for income. You can only imagine how demeaning this was for him. It surely put a strain on their relationship.

What parent would not be ecstatic over having their child healed? You would certainly expect that in this situation. Their child, blind from birth, is now completely cured. As you read the passage, you can see that the parents are quite subdued in their response to this miracle. When they are called to testify to their son's healing, they refuse to defend or have any knowledge of the situation. They were afraid of the Jewish leaders who had decided to put anyone out of the synagogue who acknowledged that Jesus was the Christ. They were more concerned about social standing in the community than the miraculous healing of their son. How sad it is when we are controlled by peer pressure. Does social acceptance keep you from telling others about Jesus? Does your witness for Christ change depending on the crowd you are in at the moment? Are you more concerned about conforming than reforming and informing others about Jesus? **Jesus needs disciples who will not be blinded by peer pressure.**

The response of our last group of people is probably the most revealing. John 9:13–34 describes the attitudes of the religious leaders. These leaders cannot deny that a man born blind has been miraculously healed. But instead of recognizing it, they attempt to undermine the obvious. They first complain that the miracle was performed on the Sabbath, as if that somehow made it invalid or unacceptable. They claimed Jesus was a sinner for doing it. The blind man's response was straightforward and to the point: "Whether he is a sinner or not, I don't know. One thing I do know. I was blind but now I see!" Their response was vicious and revealed who was truly blind. They hurled insults at the formerly blind man and had him thrown out of their meeting. It is hard to believe that men who were supposedly the religious elite of the day would respond in such a way. It demonstrates the destructive nature of legalism.

This episode reveals several truths about legalism. With legalism there is always a loss of compassion. When you read this text you can feel the coldness of the leaders. Their love had been replaced by the letter of the law (and as is typically the case, a distortion of it). With legalism there is always a loss of power for radical change. There is also a loss of faith, vision and genuine courage. Instead of encouraging total commitment, it breeds an attitude of outward conformity but little inward change. One of the most frightening aspects of legalism is that it puts a cap on commitment and openness. People exchange living the truth and being changed by it for simply knowing what's true. To help them, **Jesus needs disciples who are not blinded by legalism.**

This story reveals that the only one who could really see was the blind man. The others were blinded to the purposes of God by superficiality, peer pressure or legalism. Let's make sure our eyes stay open as we strive to follow Jesus and share him with the world.

LIFE APPLICATION

1. Are you superficial with neighbors? Do you know them well? Have they been in your home for a meal?

2. Are relatives astonished at they way you have changed? If not, what might be the reasons why?

3. Has legalistic attitudes blinded you to God's power? Are there ways you have exchanged knowing the truth for living the truth?

·7·
The Divine Position
The Widow of Nain

EMILY BRINGARDNER
Orlando, Florida

Read Luke 7:11-17

When the Lord saw her, his heart went out to her and he said, "Don't cry."

Luke 7:13

I imagine the funeral processional as they approach the city gate to bury the dead man. In that coffin are the dashed hopes of a mother.

We don't know how long it had been since she walked this same route to bury her husband. We do know she was a widow, and this was her only son; a mother who had lost her husband now had lost her son. All the "what ifs" or "might have beens" were now in vain, for he was gone.

A mother was alone and crying.

I heard that same crying the night my brother died. It was a Friday night after a high school football game. I remember getting the phone call that there had been a car accident. I was sipping hot chocolate and talking with my mom when we both heard my dad ask someone on the phone, "Both occupants of the Volkswagen?" Dad hung up the phone and very quietly said, "Ron and Elaine are dead."

And then I heard my mother cry.

And I couldn't say, "Don't cry." I remember holding her tightly and quoting every Bible verse I could remember. My heart ached for her, and I longed for her to have no reason to cry, but I knew she had reason…and I had no power to remove the reason.

I was fifteen and had been to many funerals before. But this one was different. This was my brother—the one who gave me twelve valentines when I wasn't yet in school and I didn't get valentines from classmates like my older sister did. The one who used to tell me I was special. The one who'd given me his guitar and taught me to enjoy music and theater. And most of all, the prize of my mother's heart—her firstborn. The one she was both Mom and Dad to during the World War II years. The one she struggled with and prayed for during his difficult teen years. Then, there he was—a senior in college, newly married and so full of life and promise. His life had ended, and the promises could not be kept.

This funeral processional was different because I was personally involved. I was vulnerable, but not by choice.

The Choice of Love

Here is where I stand in awe of Jesus. He chose to be vulnerable to everyone's pain. His heart ached for a woman whom he had never met. It was a simultaneous thing for him: "When he saw...his heart went out to her" with no reserve. By nature, Jesus was involved, compelled. He saw a woman he had never seen before, and immediately he felt her pain. And he did not just go about his own business.

I am reminded of the contrasting view expressed by W. H. Auden in his poem "Musée des Beaux Arts":

> About suffering they were never wrong,
> The Old Masters: how well they understood
> Its human position; how it takes place
> While someone else is eating, or opening
>   a window, or just walking dully along.

Yes, this describes the "human position." One suffers while another does a mundane task, unaware of the suffering of the other. I am so thankful for the contrast of the "Divine position." I treasure the comfort of knowing that Jesus cared when my mother cried and that Jesus is never oblivious to my pain. While he felt the joy of someone else's baby's birth, at the same exact time, he felt my pain of miscarrying our first baby at four months. While he felt the happiness of someone else's wedding vow, at the same moment he felt my sadness as I held my dying mother's hand in the intensive care unit of the hospital and promised with my sister to "take care of Dad." While Jesus' heart rejoiced at someone's engagement celebration, his heart went out to my family as we made my father's funeral arrangements. Realizing this gives me a glimpse into the unfathomable depth of the heart of Jesus. This is God's omnipresence.

Jesus' compassion knows no bounds; he has an unlimited capacity for caring, as Paul describes in Ephesians 3:18: "how wide and long and high and deep is the love of Christ." Jesus did what only he could do to ease her pain. He said, "Don't cry." What precious words to hear from the very lips of Jesus! How she must have let those words echo in her mind until her dying day, and how she must have recounted them over and over to her son when she got him back. She got him back! Amazing! A gift from the very heart of God. He did not just tell her "Don't cry." By his action, he gave her a reason to rejoice, just as he would one day give his own mother—and all of us—a reason to rejoice through his own death and resurrection.

There was no burial outside the city gates in Nain that day—only a mother rejoicing in hope.

The heart of Jesus is touched as he sees and feels our pain. Just as this woman felt the love and hope brought to her life that day, so can we. Though Jesus will not always remove the source of our pain, he will always support us and love us as we go through it. And he will remind us of the home he has prepared for us where there will be no death, no tears and no pain.

LIFE APPLICATION

1. In our own strength we are limited in how many we let our heart go out to. But are you praying to stretch the capacity of your heart to feel deeply with many others?

2. I've felt my own heart harden at times when I knew I should be feeling deeply for another person. I've had to stop and ask myself (and let others ask me), "Are you afraid of hurting? Is your lack of openness (rooted in fear of the sin of pride) blocking your passion and compassion?" How do you respond to these same questions?

3. Many years ago as I drove my son to baseball practice, an ambulance raced past us, and I asked my son to pray with me for the people in distress. I am praying to be more like Jesus in my sensitivity to the pain and suffering of those close to me, as well as to strangers. Do you need to pray this also?

·8·
The Call of the Wild
The Gerasene Demoniac

HENRY KREITE
Kelowna, British Columbia, Canada

Read Mark 5:1-20

> When Jesus got out of the boat, a man with an evil spirit came from the tombs to meet him. This man lived in the tombs, and no one could bind him any more, not even with a chain. For he had often been chained hand and foot, but he tore the chains apart and broke the irons on his feet. No one was strong enough to subdue him. Night and day among the tombs and in the hills he would cry out and cut himself with stones.
>
> Mark 5:2-5

The visuals are awesome! *He has matted, bug-infested hair. The smell of sweat and urine and excrement are clinging to his rough skin. Infected skin. The smell sickens. A torrent of blasphemous and filthy language is flowing from a mouth dripping with foam and spit. He's hunched on his knees in a darkened chamber among tombs, smashing a rock against the remnants of the shackles on his arms and legs. Here, among the dead, the monotonous pounding of the chains and his constant moaning reminds all within earshot of this man's utter misery. He is wild-eyed, cursing and screaming at everything that moves.*

Now we see the madman screaming and running naked, full-speed toward Jesus! His disciples jump behind him, afraid. Everyone is in motion, except Jesus. The man makes eye contact with Jesus, then stops as if dead. The demons bow down to Jesus. They answer Jesus. The demons inside beg Jesus, submit to Jesus, obey Jesus. And the demoniac is now a man again—healed by Jesus. What absolute power! What majesty! Someone gets the man some clothes. He is at peace. Now he is begging to be with Jesus. But Jesus tells him something and he leaves. At one time it seems everyone is begging Jesus—the demons, the man and all in the crowd.

God Can Do It

There are several great lessons within this account: the value of one soul; people are more important than things (and pigs); sometimes change can be scary for others; and real gratitude means sharing Jesus with ten cities (not just ten people). However, for me, the most obvious lesson is: *No one is beyond the reach of God!* What men can't do, what drugs can't do, what self-help books, doctors and dead religions can't do, what family and friends, and even we can't do, God can do!

A slow reading of the whole context (Mark 4:35-5:43) reveals four problems in one continuous narrative that Jesus overcame: storm, demon-possession, sickness and death. The intent, I believe, is to overwhelm us with awe. No problem is beyond Jesus. He is able to meet any need, in any person, in any sphere of creation: natural, physical, spiritual, life or death—all of them—in an absolute manner. Nothing is beyond his help. It wasn't *just* a storm he calmed, but a storm so violent even seasoned and gnarly fishermen got scared. It wasn't *just* a sick woman—her disease, pronounced incurable, socially and physically incapacited her and had cost everything she had. It wasn't *just* a dying girl. This child was stone-cold dead. The mourners were there to prove it. And it wasn't *just* any old demon possession—it was an utterly grotesque kind—a *legion* of demons making the man unapproachable and unrestrainable.

Over the years, I have seen with my own eyes such radical changes in the lives of so many disciples that it is forever impossible not to believe in the power and mercy of God. I have seen the totally depraved set free by truth and love. I have seen bizarre behavior (an animal serial killer) redeemed to a powerful and selfless life. I have known men in Africa, who once had obeyed the most wretched dictates of juju witch doctors, yet now have become awesome dads and husbands in the Lord. I have known men full of a hatred so deep it could be felt, finally forgive and embrace their enemy as a brother. And two years ago, after I thought I'd heard it all, a young man confessed a sin to me so heinous that I vomited. He, too, is now on his way to heaven!

Nothing and no one intimidates Jesus. But how often have we given up on or stopped praying for others too soon? How often have we prejudged how someone would respond to the Gospel and never even shared it with them? Have we felt in our hearts their problems and personalities were just too ugly, their philosophies too far out, or their sins too deep for God's great mercy?

Two evenings before I wrote these words, I said what turned out to be my final goodbye to a dear friend in Toronto. He had AIDS and was about to fall asleep in Christ. In 1985 I invited him to the first service of our newly planted church in Toronto. He came without reservation, but when we started to study the Bible, I discovered he was the most sexually promiscuous man I had ever met. He was a total prisoner of sin—sin of the darkest kind. Our relationship was abrasive to the point of emotional exhaustion. But, like the song says, we fought on, we fought on. His conversion was a fight to the bitter end—but he made it. He even left the church once. But, after eleven years, like Paul, he has finished the race and is in paradise with God. Before he died, he told me his only regret was not being able to serve the Christians anymore, which he so loved to do. He was (and is) a wonderful person, a gracious and tireless servant. We exchanged a few tender words, cried and said goodbye. I'll never forget that phone call.

A Modern Day Demoniac

I also knew another young man who seemed at the point of no return. He dressed oddly: long hair, black velvet platform shoes with gold flame toes, a trench coat and jeans with so many patches they weren't jeans any more. He was a blasphemer by design. He entered church buildings and screamed out curse words. He punched his fist through a stained-glass window at a convent while drunk. He was always spouting off weird ideas about things like pyramids, astral travel, *Alice in Wonderland* and white Carlos Castenada magic. He would destroy things just for fun—buildings and sometimes living things. Once he and some friends broke every window in a newly constructed school. Sometimes he set things on fire. He was in trouble with the police. He had a terrible temper and often was kicked out of athletic events. He stabbed someone with a pen. He broke into cars. He started taking LSD (green frog) when he was barely twelve years old and continued over the next six years with all kinds of other drugs—first monthly, then weekly, then daily. He spent entire paychecks on hashish, paying ten dollars for rent and sleeping on the floor of a commune. He was immoral, foulmouthed, reckless and irreverent.

But, thank God, someone gave *me* a Bible! (Yes, *me*!) A Bible, a true friend, a little patience and a lot of prayer were what it took to change my heart, my purpose and ultimately my eternity. *No one is beyond the reach of God!*

Thank God that Jesus is bound by no man's sin. Thank God that he has the power to free those who are most enslaved.

LIFE APPLICATION

1. Have you ever thought that someone was beyond even God's reach? What does that say about your view of God?

2. What changes can you make to show that you are no longer limiting how God can work?

3. In your own life, have you wondered if something was beyond God's reach? What is the truth?

· 9 ·

From Compliment to Confrontation
Nicodemus

JOHN MANNEL
St. Louis, Missouri

Read John 3:1-21

>   Now there was a man of the Pharisees named Nicodemus, a member of the Jewish ruling council. He came to Jesus at night and said, "Rabbi, we know you are a teacher who has come from God. For no one could perform the miraculous signs you are doing if God were not with him."
>   In reply Jesus declared, "I tell you the truth, no one can see the kingdom of God unless he is born again."
>
> John 3:1-3

Jesus' ministry was moving. His impact was growing. He had chosen his Twelve Apostles, performed miracles and cleared the temple. Then one night a man named Nicodemus approached him. Why did he come under the cover of darkness? Speculation abounds, but one fact remains: He did come. As hard as it may have been for a Pharisee, he did come.

We know that Jesus' days were full days. He was up before dawn to pray (Mark 1:35), then on his feet walking from place to place, calling men to follow him and teaching those who would listen. He spent hours healing the sick and confronting those who worked so hard to discredit him. But now it was night, a time for peace and rest. The Bible doesn't tell us where the disciples were at the time. Knowing them (Matthew 26:40-43) and us, we might guess that they were sleeping, understandably exhausted from the day's events, as Jesus must also have been.

Nic at Night

Jesus knew that some people's needs could be quickly dealt with: "Heal my blindness and I'll go," or "Let me just touch your garment." But when Nicodemus, a Pharisee, a religious leader and teacher, arrived at the door wanting to ask Jesus some questions, Jesus may have known that this would be a long night!

Nicodemus was a man looking for something. He had grown up learning about God, but like many then and now, he was surrounded by a system caught up in traditions and legalistic religion. Jesus, his works and his "new teaching" had captured this man's attention, and his head may have been swimming with questions: *Could this be right? Could the people who taught me so carefully not understand? Could this man be the Messiah?*

Most likely all the religion he was immersed in was the only thing he had known and seemed to him like the "right thing," but something in him must have said that there must be more. Can you relate to Nicodemus? I can. I, too, grew up religious. I knew the Bible stories and was active in my church. It wasn't until I was older that I began to recognize that there was an emptiness inside that I did not know how to fill.

As a young man, I went to the chapel at the naval base in Norfolk, Virginia, where I was stationed and sat in the empty auditorium wanting to do something, anything to connect with God, but I didn't even know how to pray. I left with an even greater void in my heart than when I'd entered.

I don't know how long it took Nicodemus to reach the point of actually going to Jesus. It took me years. He knew there was something dramatically different about Jesus' life, and he was motivated to find out what it was. His approach was relatively simple and positive: "Rabbi, we know you are a teacher who has come from God" (John 3:2a). Jesus' almost cryptic response, however, seems blunt and unappreciative in comparison: "I tell you the truth. No one can see the kingdom of God unless he is born again" (John 3:3). Jesus knew what he was doing. This man needed a wake-up call.

The conversation deepened, and before it was over Nicodemus had learned a lesson people still need to learn today: We all need a new birth, or else we will never enter the kingdom of God. Growing up in a religion and rising to the head of the class will not make us right with God. Jesus stayed with Nicodemus through his confusion and his questions until he had learned what it really took to be with God.

Looking at Nicodemus, Jesus was again reminded of religion gone wrong. Legalism had evolved from people following rules without seeking the heart of God. People were trying to earn what God desired to just give them. Jesus could have sent Nicodemus away with a sharp rebuke—after all, it was night and he was tired—but that wasn't the way of God.

Never Too Late

At the time of this writing, I was reaching out to a neighbor who had been to church a few times and has begun to study the Bible with me. A few nights before I wrote these words, the phone rang at 3:45 a.m. It was my neighbor, wanting to talk. I got up, went to his apartment and listened for hours as he told me of the pain in his life. He looked at me and said, "Many people call me to just talk, but when I needed someone, I didn't know who to call except you." I felt my heart filling with emotion as I realized the depth of our friendship. It is amazing that he trusted me enough to confide in me about his life after only a few months. What if I had not been there? What if I had not answered the phone? What if I had not been willing to get up, get dressed and get out?

Nicodemus knew he could get time with Jesus, and he did. He was taught one-on-one by the master. His questions were received and answered. He was taught the depth of God's love and was given a vision for his life. "Whoever lives by the truth comes into the light," Jesus told him (John 3:21). It wasn't until I was thirty years old that I began to earnestly seek God. Until that time, the emptiness and pain in my life continued to grow. But now I thank God for those very feelings because they woke me up and caused a search that led me to God. When I approached God out of the darkness of my night, he was there. And through his mighty power and his disciples, he took the time to fill the void in my heart with love.

Jesus still waits for eager seekers. He still tells them the truth. He still loves them. He still shows them how to end an old life and begin a new one.

LIFE APPLICATION

1. Remember when you first became a disciple. Who was instrumental in answering your questions and helping you to see the truth? What sacrifices do you see that they made for you? Are you doing the same for others around you?

2. When the phone rings late at night, do you answer it? Examine your heart for limits and conditions you have put on serving and giving. How will you go about tearing these down? What are some very practical steps you can take, starting today?

3. Who are your religious friends? How are you helping them come to a saving faith? If you can't think of any, pray that God will use you in this way soon.

•10•
The Price Is Always Higher; the Cost Is Always Greater; and the Work Is Always Harder
Three Men Called to Discipleship

TONEY MULHOLLAN
Spring, Texas

> As they were walking along the road, a man said to him, "I will follow you wherever you go."
> Jesus replied, "Foxes have holes and birds of the air have nests, but the Son of Man has no place to lay his head."
> He said to another man, "Follow Me."
> But the man replied, "Lord, first let me go and bury my father."
> Jesus said to him, "Let the dead bury their own dead, but you go and proclaim the kingdom of God."
> Still another said, "I will follow you, Lord; but first let me go back and say goodbye to my family."
> Jesus replied, "No one who puts his hand to the plow and looks back is fit for service in the kingdom of God."
>
> Luke 9:57-62

The religious world often paints the Christian walk as easy and characterized by prosperity, wellness and happiness. This attitude has filtered into the church and unfortunately, into the thought life of many disciples. In contrast, Jesus describes a life that is truly blessed, but filled with many challenges and genuine hardships. In light of that, Luke 9:57-62, is one of the most neglected passages in all of Scripture.

Each time I read this passage it turns my head, shocks my senses and challenges my discipleship. This is not the Jesus of my childhood—meek and mild and always ready to comfort and console. This is a Jesus who challenges my conceptions of the kingdom and what it means to follow him. I'm sure my feelings are similar to the reaction that these three individuals experienced even as they volunteered to follow Jesus. Let's examine these encounters and listen to the deep lessons Jesus is teaching them and us.

1. It's Not As Easy As It Looks
Matthew 8:18 (a parallel passage) identifies the first man as a teacher of the law. This group was generally opposed to the ministry of Jesus. Yet this man volunteers to give up his association and follow Jesus wherever he goes. Teachers of the law were generally held in high regard and well respected. What a great opportunity Jesus had to expand the influence of his ministry: to actually convert one of his detractors. But instead of welcoming in this new follower with open arms, Jesus warns him of the sacrifices that lie ahead. Jesus tells him, "Foxes have holes and birds of the air have nests, but the Son of Man has no place to lay his head" (Luke 9:58).

What point was Jesus making with his challenging response? Jesus is saying that following him is not as easy as it looks. Jesus did not want the man to operate under the delusion that things were going to be easy. Jesus wanted him to know that discipleship was hard work and even the security of having a place to call home was not to be counted on.

What is the lesson for us? Discipleship does not promise a life of comfort—it promises quite the opposite. Jesus spends much of his ministry calling his followers to a life of self-denial, taking up a cross and forsaking their own interest. He summarizes that heart of following him when he says, "Whoever loses his life for me will save it" (Luke 9:24).

2. Life and Death Matters

The second man who volunteers to follow receives a greater challenge than the first. Jesus calls this man to follow him, and the man desires to, but his father has passed away and he needs to bury him. Surely, if there was ever a legitimate excuse for delaying discipleship, this was it. Even in the face of this sorrowful event, Jesus says, "Let the dead bury their own dead, but you go and proclaim the kingdom of God." It seems insensitive, perhaps even callous. Yet, in this one statement Jesus provides a stark contrast between matters of life and death! Jesus teaches in other places the importance of caring for others, just as he made sure his mother was cared for as he was being crucified. But in this statement Jesus shows the supremacy of life that is offered when we proclaim the kingdom of God. This call to proclaim the kingdom and to share the good news of Jesus is our call to one of the most important things we will do as disciples. It is not optional or only for those who are gifted. Jesus makes it clear and indisputable that proclamation of the kingdom of God is serious and supreme! Let us proclaim Christ and give life to our world.

3. No Looking Back

The third individual also agrees to follow Jesus but immediately attaches a stipulation to it. He tells Jesus he must first go back and say farewell to his family. Jesus replies, "No one who puts his hand to the plow and looks back is fit for service in the kingdom of God." I think Jesus is making it plain that no stipulations can be attached to following him. Our commitment to him must be total and unconditional.

The people listening to Jesus would have recognized his allusion to the ministry of Elijah and his calling of Elisha (read 1 Kings 19:19–21). Elijah honored Elisha's request to go and say goodbye to his family before he began his apprenticeship as a prophet. Jesus was making it known that his calling to discipleship was more urgent and immediate.

Jesus says if we are looking back and still longing for the

things of the world, we are not "fit for service" in the kingdom. He is calling for a heart that is undivided and is looking ahead, not behind.

Jesus promises an abundant life to every follower, but not the kind of abundance the world offers. These encounters teach us that when it comes to following Jesus, the price is always higher, the cost is always greater, and the work is always harder.

LIFE APPLICATION

1. It's natural that as we age we seek comfort. Society says, we've earned retirement, it's our time to kick back and relax. How does that fit in with Jesus' call to sacrifice and to follow his example?

2. Has the proclaimation of the gospel become an optional endeavor in your life? Is it relegated to a few special invitations a month or even a year? What decisions will it take, to again make it a priority in your lifestyle and in your ministry?

3. Have your compartmentalized your commitment to Jesus? Are there aspects of the Christian life that you refuse to grow in? Do you neglect sharing your faith because it is uncomfortable? Is your monetary giving anemic or only present when you have surplus funds? Is helping the poor, or visiting the sick, for people who have the time or the inclination?

4. As your survey your life, in what areas are you taking your hands off the plow and looking back? What steps of repentance do you need to take to advance the cause of Christ in your life and in the world?

·11·
He Looked at Him and Loved Him
The Rich Young Ruler

FRANÇOIS AND PENNY FAURE

> *Read Luke 18:18-29*
>
> When Jesus heard this, he said to him, "You still lack one thing. Sell everything you have and give to the poor, and you will have treasure in heaven. Then come, follow me."
> When he heard this, he became very sad, because he was a man of great wealth. Jesus looked at him and said, "How hard it is for the rich to enter the kingdom of God!"
>
> Luke 18:22-24

When Jesus first met this man, it seemed like the perfect opportunity.

"A certain ruler asked him, 'Good teacher, what must I do to inherit eternal life?'" Wouldn't all disciples love to meet somebody who comes across as this man does initially? He is young (Matthew 19:22), influential, open and eager. Our thoughts and mouths would be racing: "Of course, I will tell you how to inherit eternal life. Let's meet at my place tonight, and we can study the Bible together!" Jesus, however, had a very different response to the rich young ruler. Instead of a warm welcome, he greets him sternly with a question: "Why do you call me good? No one is good except God alone" (Luke 18:19). Did the man know what he was saying? Was he prepared to acknowledge Jesus as God?

Challenge

The challenge Jesus gives the young man—to sell everything and follow him—really amounts to "It's not what you do but who you are." It reflects a heart set fully on following Jesus, and for this man it meant a willingness to sell all. I (Penny) remember when I, as an Australian, was challenged while studying the Bible to stay in France, because of various needs in the church. Living in France had never been part of my plan, and François was very keen to live in Australia. He showed little interest in studying the Bible himself. I was trying to have a spiritual perspective, which meant being willing to do anything to encourage François to start studying the Bible. I overcame my struggle; we decided to stay and nine months later François became a Christian. The blessings have never ceased. I am so grateful that someone challenged me as Jesus would have.

Rich in Love

When we meet the rich young ruler in Mark's gospel, we find him on his knees before Jesus after running up to him to ask how he might inherit eternal life. As we follow the exchange, it soon becomes clear that, despite his earnestness, this man is out of touch with himself and God. If we had met him ourselves, we would be excited at first but then quickly angry and frustrated with his self-righteous and prideful answers. We might think, but not say: *Who do you think you are? Obeying all the commands always—we don't think so. Take a good look in the mirror!* And Mark tells us that Jesus did challenge him, but Jesus also loved him. Jesus uncompromisingly pointed this young man to the narrow way, yet at the same time he drew close to him, wanting to give him strength, faith and hope. How many times after challenging someone have we felt joy at their repentance but also a deep shame knowing what was really in our hearts and minds? We have thoughts like: *How many times have we talked about this and still no change? How could she do, say, think that as a disciple?*

We were were studying the Bible with a couple who have been living together for more than four years and were planning to be married within two months. I (Penny) spoke to the woman about loving God more than her fiancé and about the idea of their moving into two separate apartments. It was not an easy decision since they had recently found a new apartment, but they did move apart. She even called me on the phone this week to ask for my forgiveness because she had had some lingering bad attitudes about the challenge. We dealt with it quickly, and both of us realized that when we feel loved, it is so much easier to "swallow" the truth.

Perspective

In answering this rich young man's question, Jesus does not get into a lengthy discussion or theological debate. He knows that our problem—sin—resides in the heart, not the head. He saw deeper into this man's heart than the man himself had ever seen. He saw areas of weakness the man needed to deal with if he was going to enter the kingdom of heaven. Jesus simply wanted this man to see and acknowledge his sin.

Each of us lacks that "one thing" deep down that we must give up if we want to follow Jesus. Sometimes we don't even know exactly what it is ourselves, but enough time in God's word will certainly reveal it (Hebrews 4:12-13).

Jesus' words challenged the ruler with the commandments that would eventually make him aware of his own sin. The man left sad and convicted, aware of all that he lacked: earthly poverty and spiritual riches. It is hard to leave Jesus feeling justified in our arrogance and pride. How do people leave us? To be like Jesus we must get to the heart.

LIFE APPLICATION

1. Are you sometimes tempted to give in to someone's outward righteousness and to water down the conviction that all have sinned (Romans 3:23) and need to humbly repent?

2. How do people leave our homes after a chal-lenging time? Do they leave feeling justified in their arrogance because of our lack of conviction or lack of knowledge? Or do they leave humbled and convicted before God?

3. When are you tempted to not love those you need to challenge? What attitude or sin on their part is most likely to cause you to withdraw emotionally? Decide today to do everything it takes to remain loving, even through challenging times. (See 2 Timothy 2:24-26.)

4. How can you better prepare for moments like Jesus spent with the rich young ruler, understanding that this very time could determine someone's eternal destiny?

·12·
Dinnertime Discipling
The Twelve Apostles

TONEY MULHOLLAN
Spring, Texas

A dispute also arose among them as to which of them was considered to be greatest. Jesus said to them, "The kings of the Gentiles lord it over them; and those who exercise authority over them call themselves Benefactors. But you are not to be like that. Instead, the greatest among you should be like the youngest, and the one who rules like the one who serves. For who is greater, the one who is at the table or the one who serves? Is it not the one who is at the table? But I am among you as one who serves. You are those who have stood by me in my trials. And I confer on you a kingdom, just as my Father conferred one on me, so that you may eat and drink at my table in my kingdom and sit on thrones, judging the twelve tribes of Israel.

"Simon, Simon, Satan has asked to sift all of you as wheat. But I have prayed for you, Simon, that your faith may not fail. And when you have turned back, strengthen your brothers."

Luke 22:24–32

While I was growing up, it was the one meal you never missed. Breakfast or lunch could be side-stepped, but you always made it home for dinner. It was more than just eating together; it was the time when eight family members worked out conflicts, shared joys and imperceptibly gained strength that comes from shared love and common heritage.

Jesus powerfully used mealtimes with his disciples, and none stand out more poignantly than does this final Passover meal. No event in Jesus' ministry captures so clearly his' love and vision for his closest followers as this dinner shaped by love and devotion.

At this meal in an upper room, Jesus addressed topics that would be essential to the growth of these men and for our growth. And foundational to these concerns, he displayed the attitude that would bind them together and provide the driving force to make them a reality. Let's examine these four key ingredients.

1) Loyalty. "You are those who have stood by me in my trials" (Luke 22:28, also 22:20–23). Jesus commends the disciples for their loyalty. Few character traits are more highly valued (by those who receive it) than loyalty. This treasured virtue has become almost extinct in our world and, unfortunately, even among Christians.

Loyalty is important to a great Christian life, and Jesus taught its value on several occasions. Even in this final supper Jesus exemplifies loyalty. He would be the ultimate example of it—for Jesus knew that not only would Judas betray him, but every man at the table, his closest friends, would desert him. How many of us could love, extend loyalty and gently instruct friends who we knew would shortly betray us!

2) Service Instead of Position. "But I am among you as one who serves" (Luke 22:27b; see also 22:24–27a). Jesus speaks even more powerfully on this topic than the first. For the disciples were drawn to the seductive promises of power that so many in our world have devoted their lives to today. The world lauds power as a worthy goal, while Jesus insists that greatness comes from the joy of serving others instead of ourselves.

Even as Jesus' disciples struggled with this temptation, he called them to follow his example. Our call to service is demonstrated powerfully by Jesus. At a time when he should have been the one to be served, he showed them the full extent of his love by wrapping a towel around his waist, getting on his knees and washing the feet of his disciples. This was not a symbolic gesture; it was an act that was typical of Jesus ministry' among the men he was training for ministry.

A genuine leader of God's people doesn't need authority to lead—he needs power to serve. Jesus' most ardent instructions are left for these closing hours of his ministry as he challenges his men to aspire to serve and not to garner positions of power. Even as he conferred a kingdom on them he insisted that service would be a hallmark of it: "Instead, the greatest among you should be like the youngest, and the one who rules like the one who serves....I am among you as one who serves" (Luke 22:26-27).

3) A Kingdom Purpose. "And I confer on you a kingdom" (Luke 22:29). It's not uncommon in the busy activity of the Christian life to lose sight of our true purpose. When Jesus initially called these men it was to become fishers of men and to bring people into the kingdom. In these final hours he reminds them of this purpose and will do so again before his return to heaven (Matthew 28:18-20). It is crucial that each of us remind ourselves of the privilege of introducing others into God's kingdom.

4) Addressing Specific Sins. "But I have prayed for you, Simon, that your faith may not fail" (Luke 22:32). It is a great temptation to generalize our teaching and avoid specific application to ourselves or others—a temptation that Jesus did not give in to. Jesus used this hour to address a serious sin in Peter's life, but also to pray for him and give him a vision that he could change. Specific application produced a leader who dramatically changed and helped the good news spread around the world.

We must not hesitate in addressing our own sins and the sins of others. When we speak up, God can use it to build men and women who will love, serve and change our world.

Bound Together by Love

Jesus speaks masterfully on these four issues, but the ingredient that makes his lesson so powerful is love. Jesus speaks of loyalty while the men he addresses are about to become the ultimate object lessons of disloyalty. Jesus talks of service to disciples who in his very presence are arguing about which of them should have positions of authority. If that were not enough, Jesus confers a kingdom on a group of men who are cowards, betrayers and deserters. Then, he crowns these acts by expressing faith in their strongest leader who was about to publicly deny any association with him.

Jesus saw beyond the failures of the past and through the sins of the present. Our willingness to love and believe in others is usually predicated on a person's past and present performance. Because of this we struggle to believe in ourselves and others. We become prisoners of the past and lose vision for how God can change us. Truly, when love is waning, our vision for others weakens. But even when we doubt, Jesus still loves and has faith in what we can become.

We must restore the quality of love that Jesus so effectively shared with his disciples. It is not easy and it takes returning to a Jesus kind of love and addressing these same issues that he talked about in this final meal. It is time to sit down together at dinner, take Jesus' teachings to heart and implement them with his empowering example of love.

LIFE APPLICATION

1. Do others consider you loyal? What are some of the ways you can grow in your loyalty to others?

2. Is serving others a hallmark of your leadership? Come up with a plan to serve others on a weekly basis.

3. God has conferred on you a kingdom. In what specific ways are you working to advance the kingdom of God?

4. Have you let sins go unaddressed in others and in your own life? What can you do this week to address that issue in your ministry?

•13•
God Comes Looking
The Man Blind from Birth

NANCY MANNEL
St. Louis, Missouri

Read John 9:1-41
"One thing I do know, I was blind but now I see!"
John 9:25

The man was a beggar. A poor, blind beggar. Blind from birth. There was nothing about him that would have drawn you to him. His appearance was undoubtedly like that of any homeless person found begging on the streets of Chicago, Bombay or Manila. To many he was probably considered a nuisance, a burden, a blemish to the community. I doubt that many would have stopped to chat. Most would have averted their eyes. He was someone to be avoided—after all, his blindness was punishment for some sin he or one of his parents had committed. "Rabbi, who sinned, this man or his parents, that he was born blind?" asked the disciples (John 9:2). You would think by now their concerns would be more like Jesus'. Why not ask, "What can we do to help this poor man?" or better yet, "Jesus, you have the power. Won't you heal this poor blind beggar?"

They were with him in Galilee when he healed the royal official's son (John 4:43-54). They were with him again at the pool when Jesus healed the paralyzed man (John 5:1-14). They took part in the feeding of the 5,000 with five small barley loaves and two small fish (John 6:1-15). They even witnessed Jesus walking on water (John 6:16-24).

But rather than rebuke them, Jesus saw this as an avenue not only to heal but to teach. "Neither this man nor his parents sinned, but this happened so that the work of God might be displayed in his life" (John 9:3). Jesus knew his work here on earth was quickly coming to an end. His intensity showed as he used every opportunity to teach about God's love, power and mercy.

Blind Obedience

Jesus acted, but not predictably: "He spit on the ground, made some mud with his saliva, and put it on the man's eyes" (John 9:6).

Can you imagine what must have been going through the blind man's mind? No introduction and no questions from Jesus. The man simply felt something moist and heavy being applied to his eyes. Then he hears Jesus for the first time: "Go, wash in the pool of Siloam" (John 9:7). The man simply went to the water and washed—truly "blind obedience" in this case. Then he went home with newfound sight (John 9:7). What a glorious day for this man who had been born blind!

But because it was the Sabbath, the people dragged him to the temple courts where he unfortunately spent his first few hours of sight staring at the tight, accusing faces of the Pharisees. "Who did this?" "How was it done?" "Were you *really* born blind?" Yet, the man's responses were instruc-tive and convicting.

Simple honesty: "I was blind, but now I see!" (John 9:25).

Childlike innocence: "Do you want to become his disciples too?" (John 9:27).

Boldness: "Now that's remarkable! You don't know where he comes from, yet he opened my eyes. We know that God does not listen to sinners. He listens to the godly man who does his will" (John 9:30-31).

Just that morning, Jesus had no doubt told some of these same people: "For I know where I came from and where I am going. But you have no idea where I come from or where I am going" (John 8:14). Maybe Jesus was making one more attempt through this healing to help the Pharisees see how blind they really were.

After hearing that the Pharisees had thrown the man out of

the temple, Jesus went looking for him. "Do you believe in the Son of Man?" Jesus asked (John 9:35). Since the man addressed him as "Sir," we can only assume he did not yet recognize Jesus as the one who had opened his eyes.

But again the humility of the man's heart is revealed when Jesus identified himself and immediately the man proclaimed: "'Lord, I believe,' and he worshipped him" (John 9:38). Jesus did more than open a blind man's eyes that day; he opened his heart as well. He not only gave the man his sight; he gave him his life!

Biblical Blindness

Studying Jesus with the man born blind has helped me to understand my own "spiritual blindness." I was raised in a religious home. I believed in God and Jesus and the cross. I always went to church. I sang in the choir, went to Sunday School, spent several summers at church camp and was even president of my youth group. I certainly looked like a "good Christian." But I was blind to what it meant to have a close and committed relationship with God (Luke 9:23).

It wasn't until many years later, after I was married and had two children, that I realized how far away from God I was. With my life empty and my marriage falling apart, I still did not really look for God, but thankfully God came looking for me! He sent two wonderful people into my life: Roger and Marcia Lamb* shared their love, their lives, their hearts and their knowledge of the Scriptures with me. Within a few months, I was led to my pool of Siloam where I was washed in the waters of baptism and came home forgiven.

John and I have been married almost 50 years. Our children are all dedicated disciples and Jesus Christ has made a tremendous impact on all of our family.

Jesus did not see people as objects for theological discussions. He saw them as persons with needs. Find someone in your world who is blind or disabled. Don't discuss them. Reach out and love them.

LIFE APPLICATION

1. Have you made it easy for Jesus to find you?

2. How do you respond when questioned about your spiritual beliefs?

3. Have you been to the Pool of Siloam so that you can be given a new life? If so, what was it like when you came up out of the water and first opened your "new" eyes?

4. Who do you know who is "blind" and hurting and needs the touch of the Christ?

*You can read this couple's remarkable story in their book *This Doesn't Feel Like Love: Trusting God When Bad Things Happen* (Spring, Texas: Illumination Publishers, 2016, available at www.ipibooks.com).

·14·
A Friend of Sinners
Zaccheaus

GREG AND SHELLEY METTEN
Marina del Rey, California

> Zacchaeus, come down immediately. I must stay at your house today."
>
> Luke 19:5

During Jesus' life on earth, people were his all-consuming passion and joy. He taught them, walked with them and reclined with them over a leisurely meal. He enjoyed being with all types of people from every conceivable walk of life. It did not matter if they were rich or poor, educated or illiterate, healthy or sick, Jew or Gentile—there was not one ounce or milligram of prejudice in his heart. Jesus understood people's hearts. He knew how much he could expect from them. And his expectations were based on the spiritual condition of each individual's heart.

A Call Higher

Zacchaeus was a man everyone loved to hate. He exemplified everything that was wrong with the world: greed, corruption and self-indulgence. He was shunned by his fellow Jews and exploited by the Roman authorities for whom he collected taxes. When he heard that Jesus was passing through town, he wanted to see him. When his money apparently could not buy him an audience with Jesus, he did something surely uncharacteristic for a man in his position: He climbed a tree to get a glimpse of the man who was rumored to be having such a tremendous impact.

When Jesus glanced up and saw Zacchaeus perched precariously in the tree, it must have brought a smile to his face. The effort impressed Jesus, and he called him: "Zacchaeus, come down immediately. I must stay at your house today" (Luke 19:5). Jesus' straightforward approach may have offended some, but Zacchaeus "welcomed him gladly" (19:6). We can easily imagine Jesus walking Zacchaeus home, talking, even laughing and having vision for his newfound friend. Jesus thoroughly enjoyed people. He didn't view them as problems or inconveniences, but rather, as individuals.

We need to learn how to enjoy people as Jesus did. Too often our hectic lifestyles and wrong attitudes keep us from being refreshed and stimulated by the different kinds and types of relationships God opens up for us. Sometimes we only see people as projects, and we go about working on them in a very businesslike fashion. Jesus saw each person as a unique creation. Yes, people were challenging, but they were also exciting, full of potential and possibilities. Whether speaking to Nicodemus at night or conversing for a few minutes with the Samaritan woman at the well, Jesus made friends with people easily. To be more like him, we must decide to let down our guard, be ourselves and just have fun with people. If the desire is there, and the prayers for wisdom have been prayed, we will find, just like Jesus did, the right words to say.

In his encounter with Zacchaeus, Jesus showed how he loved all people—no matter who they were or where they came from. He felt completely at home in the presence of all: tax collectors, prostitutes, Samaritans, lepers, demon-possessed men and fishermen. While the crowds outside were murmuring about Jesus spending time with a despicable tax collector, he was inside sharing his heart and life with a man who could change, to the glory of God.

Prejudice Robs Us

Jesus forces us to confront the intolerance we have in our hearts (sometimes hidden even to us). In September 1986, we moved to Bombay, India, to help plant the new church. The excitement of being in India was soon replaced by the reality of the enormous task of living in a land with a people who seemed so different. I (Greg) remember taking a train to one of the remote villages in order to spend time with a medical doctor with whom I was sharing my faith. As I boarded the train, four men started pushing me into the train compartment, and I knew immediately that my wallet had been stolen. I was confused and angry and had to leap off of the train, since I didn't have enough money for the rest of the journey.

As I walked the two miles home, I began in my mind to berate the Indian people about how dishonest they were and wondered why I'd ever agreed to go to India (as if there were no crime in the United States!). Suddenly, I stopped and listened to what I was telling myself. I saw the prejudice that I had allowed to form in my own heart toward the Indian people. I prayed and asked God to forgive me and fill my heart with compassion and understanding for what the people must endure. When I arrived home, I got more money and took the next train back to my friend and studied the Bible with him.

Prejudice makes us think we can relate to only those people who are like us. We start labeling others as "different" or "strange." In Los Angeles, where we now live, this is a major problem. Many communities and churches are separated by racial or socioeconomic lines. What draws people to our church services is the cross section of people from every area of society. But, we, too must always guard our hearts for attitudes that can easily creep in and cause disunity. Sometimes even disciples start murmuring about the color of a person's skin who is put into leadership rather than being thankful for his or her spiritual maturity. Jesus was looking at Zacchaeus' heart, not at the classification he had in his society.

Luke 19 does not indicate that Jesus preached a sermon or rebuked him. It does indicate that he offered him friendship and acceptance. Zacchaeus responded to Jesus' unconditional love by repenting and completely changing his life: "Look, Lord! Here and now I give half of my possessions to the poor, and if I have cheated anybody out of anything, I will pay back four times the amount" (19:8).

Jesus believed in Zacchaeus and had vision for what he could become. He shows us how very quickly a heart can be turned toward God when genuine friendship and acceptance are offered. After only a brief encounter with Jesus, Zacchaeus became a changed man. This week, call someone you know to come down from his or her "tree." Have a meal with them. Let them see the Jesus in you that will change everything for them.

LIFE APPLICATION

1. Jesus enjoyed spending time with people. How much time in your weekly schedule do you allow for times devoted to building relationships with Christians and non-Christians?

2. Are there any people you feel any prejudice toward or just feel uncomfortable being around?

3. When reaching out to people, do you find yourself building deep, meaningful friendships, or are you constantly being superficial or businesslike? Do you enjoy people and learn from them?

·15·
The Greatest in the Kingdom
The Little Children

AL AND GLORIA BAIRD
Phoenix, Arizona

> At that time the disciples came to Jesus and asked, "Who is the greatest in the kingdom of heaven?"
> He called a little child and had him stand among them. And he said: "I tell you the truth, unless you change and become like little children, you will never enter the kingdom of heaven. Therefore, whoever humbles himself like this child is the greatest in the kingdom of heaven.
> Matthew 18:1-4

> "What do you think? If a man owns a hundred sheep, and one of them wanders away, will he not leave the ninety-nine on the hills and go to look for the one that wandered off? And if he finds it, I tell you the truth, he is happier about that one sheep than about the ninety-nine that did not wander off. In the same way your Father in heaven is not willing that any of these little ones should be lost."
> Matthew 18:12-14

Jesus' attitude toward children and his words about them in Matthew 18 teach us two powerful lessons.

Become Like Children

First, we need to become like children in a very specific way. People are power freaks. Our human nature wants to be first and to have control. We get this from Satan himself, because that is his nature, too. In heaven he rebelled against God and has been rebellious ever since. The disciples in Matthew 18 were driven by this same desire to be in control when they asked Jesus: "Who is the greatest?" That was their smooth way of saying, as James and John inferred in Matthew 20, "How can I be the greatest?" Jesus, making the most of this opportunity, taught about his nature and how different it is from our sinful nature. He called a little child to him as an object lesson. Why a little child? Because Satan has not yet sunk his claws into the children and corrupted them. Jesus teaches us about his nature through them. When we become like little children, we become like Jesus. With the child in their midst, Jesus gave them the rebuke of their lives. *Because of your power-hungry pride you guys are not even in the kingdom of God, and nothing will change this fact unless you start imitating this child!*

But even this did not change them. It took several repetitions of this important lesson. And it still did not really sink in until Jesus showed his ultimate love at the cross. After his sacrifice, all of Jesus' teachings made sense in a way they had never made sense before. Because of the cross, these men made incredible changes that enabled them to turn the world upside down. And so it is with us. Having a child's humility is impossible until we understand the cross and allow it to have its impact on us. "Greater love has no one than this, that he lay down his life for his friends" (John 15:13).

Little Spiritual Children

But second, we not only need to become like children, but we must also see our brothers and sisters in Christ as God's little spiritual children who must be cared for. The heart of God is that not a single person be lost. Is that our heart? Do we feel the personal responsibility for our brothers and sisters in the church?

Studies of people who have wandered away from God in the congregation in Los Angeles indicate that one half of those who leave do so in their first four months as Christians. They are vulnerable little children, and Satan is preying on them. Mike Taliaferro, who was serving as evangelist for the great Johannesburg church, has written a gripping book, *The Lion Never Sleeps,** which addresses this problem. In it, he graphically describes how a lion stalks and kills his prey and compares it to the way Satan stalks and destroys Christians. His conclusion, which we must all take to heart, is that we are not equipping and protecting our young believers adequately.

Jesus taught in his Great Commission (Matthew 28:18-20) that, as his disciples, we are not only to make disciples, but we are to teach them (prepare them, equip them) to obey everything. Teaching obedience to Jesus is not completed in some five-lesson series; it is a lifetime project! Every one of us needs at least one significant person in our lives to teach us obedience to Jesus, someone who makes us feel "believed in." We need a person who will not only tell us what we need to hear, but a person who will also listen to what we are thinking and dealing with: the good, the bad and the ugly.

Recently, a married couple we know went through a very difficult time of doubting their love for God and each other. The wife decided that she wanted to leave and proceeded to cut herself off from all friends and all help. Gloria's repeated phone calls went unanswered. They finally did talk, and the wife stated that her relationship with God and her marriage were over. She refused to discuss it further. That night Gloria went to her house, and since no one answered the doorbell, she left her some flowers and a note on the steps. The note said simply, "I love you, and I will not give up on you. No matter what you do, I will be here for you." Two days later the woman came to our house in tears, ready to put her life and her marriage back together. Gloria's note had shown her the unconditional love and friendship that she needed. How often do we give up too soon? Perhaps what all people need is to know that someone loves them enough to come after them.

We all need someone who will love us unconditionally and who will refuse to let us walk away from God. But we also need to be that person for someone else. If God is not willing to lose a single one, then neither should we be willing. We must dig into our own hearts and feel God's pain and love for those who have strayed. We must be willing to move past our point of comfort and go the extra mile—or two or three—to find our lost brothers and sisters.

Jesus loved children. He saw in them a humility we must possess to be in the kingdom. He also saw that the children in the church (all disciples) must be loved and cared for. He shows us that "the Father in heaven is not willing that any of these little ones should be lost" (Matthew 18:14). He demonstrates the attitude that must be in our hearts.

LIFE APPLICATION

1. Which are you most like: "How great I am!" or "How worthless I am!"? Discuss this with the person who knows you best spiritually. How can that person help you find the correct balance?

2. What has made you want to give up and wander off? What kept you from leaving? What did you learn from this? How can you use this lesson to help others?

3. Think about those who have wandered off. What could you and others have done to prevent it? Did you give up on them too quickly?

4. Who do you know who is struggling spiritually? What can you do to help them? *Do it!*

*Mike Taliaferro, *The Lion Never Sleeps*. (Spring, Texas: Illumination Publishers, 2014, available at www.ipibooks.com).

•16•
No 'Dogs' in Heaven
The Canaanite Woman

SHEILA JONES
Hermitage, Tennessee

Read Matthew 15

> Leaving that place, Jesus withdrew to the region of Tyre and Sidon. A Canaanite woman from that vicinity came to him, crying out, "Lord, Son of David, have mercy on me! My daughter is suffering terribly from demon-possession."
>
> Matthew 15:21-22

A slice of the life of Jesus. After his encounter with the hardhearted Pharisees earlier in Matthew 15, the disciples had become concerned about their PR in the region: "Do you know that the Pharisees were offended when they heard this?" they queried with wide-eyed amazement (15:16).

"Are you still so dull?" he had asked.

Jesus must have realized that it was time for a retreat. Time to regroup and refuel spiritually. After all, this is the group who would bring the message to the whole world.

Retreat Time

So he left that place, Matthew tells us (15:21), withdrawing with the Twelve to the region of Tyre and Sidon, about forty miles away. He physically distanced himself for a short while from the lost sheep of Israel. He needed time with his chosen few.

Jesus tried to enter the region incognito. But word travels quickly—especially when it is the word that brings healing and hope. A woman showed up, fell desperately at the feet of Jesus and begged him to heal her daughter (15:22-28).

At first Jesus did not say anything. He did not respond at all. This interruption was not part of his build-and-bond agenda. But he had encountered many interruptions in his ministry. Of course, he didn't just see some interference; he saw hurting people, and his heart went out to them. *Why so silent in this case, Lord?* the disciples may have wondered.

Revealing the Hearts of Many

Surely the disciples had learned not to turn away anyone too quickly when they approached Jesus. Hadn't they seen his gracious response to the sinful woman who had crashed their dinner party? She defied all the customs and rules of the time to do so, but Jesus affirmed her faith and treated her tenderly. But with the Canaanite woman Jesus was silent; and by his silence he tested and revealed both the hearts of his disciples and the heart of this Gentile woman.

Did compassion live in the hearts of the disciples as they looked down at the heap of female humanity on the ground before them? Or was law, and justified responses to that law, their criteria for evaluating the situation? Perhaps the instructions given earlier by Jesus when he had sent them out two by two were fresh on their minds: "Do not go among the Gentiles... Go rather to the lost sheep of Israel" (Matthew 10:5). Perhaps they thought, *Jesus said only the lost sheep. She is not a lost sheep. Therefore, too bad. Get her out of here. Send her away. She's bugging us.* By their reaction, it seems they failed the test.

Jesus did not send her away as they asked him. He said simply, "I was sent only to the lost sheep of Israel" (15:24). A further test for the disciples and for her. Would they steel themselves against her even more as Jesus verbalized their thoughts? Would she give up? How strong was her passion, her character, her faith?

Jesus' next statement could have sent her reeling and caused her to bitterly lick her wounds: "It is not right to take the children's bread and toss it to their dogs" (15:26). This compassionate Savior was willing to be misunderstood in order to flush out faith or faithlessness in the heart of this woman, and to teach his disciples—and us—a lesson in grace. Sure, he was sent first to the Jews. And the Jews, his disciples included, looked down on the Gentiles as dogs. But, hadn't Jesus healed Gentiles from the earliest days in his ministry? (Matthew 4:24). Hadn't he been moved by the faith of the centurion, one outside the fold? Hadn't Jesus said of him, "I have not found anyone in Israel with such great faith"? (Matthew 8:10).

Was this the same Jesus who seemed to be giving this poor woman such a hard time? The Scripture says that he is "the same yesterday and today and forever" (Hebrews 13:8). His character is consistent. His compassion is consistent. Couldn't Jesus be testing the heart of a desperate woman to teach her, and to teach his disciples and us, that he hears and he answers, even when we think he isn't listening or doesn't care? We need to realize, as this woman did, that Jesus is listening and that we are not "dogs" in his sight when we ask.

Request Granted

Remarkably, Jesus affirmed her faith, even as he must have admired her grit. He didn't see her as an annoyance when she continued to beseech him. After all, he himself told the parable of the persistent widow, teaching us to keep on asking and believing.

After feeling justified in telling Jesus to send her away, the disciples must have dropped their heads and stared at the ground when Jesus granted her request. Surely they avoided her eyes, full of joy and gratitude, as she ran to see her little daughter.

Once again the unpredictable Master "revealed the hearts" of his disciples as he stepped over legalism and prejudice and rewarded a faithful heart. He did not see the woman as unsubmissive or rebellious or undeserving. He saw her only as full of faith, because he saw all the way through to her heart.

There are times when I, unlike this determined woman, think, "Yeah. I'm a dog. I'm not worthy of God answering my prayers. My faith is not strong enough. My convictions are not deep enough." My heart condemns me when Jesus does not. I need to repent and go after making changes in my life. But thank God that he does not wait for me to be "undogly" in my own eyes before he blesses me!

Jesus does not disregard our cause, even though there are always grounds to prove that he should. His grace is greater than all our sin. He hears and answers the consistent, determined, obedient prayer of faith—no matter who prays it.

LIFE APPLICATION

1. What are the grounds upon which you might build a case for Jesus not listening to you or answering your prayers? Why, biblically speaking, are these "insufficient" grounds?

2. In what situation have you been like the disciples—quick to cut someone off or to decide they were not worthy of your time and attention? Did you or do you now see the self-righteousness in such an approach to someone?

3. Jesus was more concerned about helping someone to grow in their faith than he was in keeping up a "nice-guy" image. How does this truth apply to your life?

4. List five things this story tells you about the character of Jesus.

·17·
A Crowd-Pleaser
The Bleeding Woman and Jairus' Daughter

KAREN LOUIS
Singapore

Read Luke 8:40-56
(See also Matthew 9:18-26 and Mark 5:21-43.)

> Now when Jesus returned, a crowd welcomed him, for they were all expecting him.
>
> Luke 8:40

Have you ever felt that your ministry was "a bit dry"? That it was "hard work" to bring someone to God? That you were "straining" to get people to come along to services? That it was a real effort to get Christians to even stay faithful?

We have all felt this way at times, yet we can see from the verse above that Jesus had the opposite problem! Crowds followed him to the point of his exhaustion. As his disciples, if we are not having these experiences, we must examine why. Why did Jesus' life draw a crowd?

Selfless Servant

Jesus came home after a long day. He had just taken care of "Legion," led a packed "Bible discussion group," healed a paralytic, gone evangelizing and had dinner with a bunch of "sinners" (Matthew 8:28-9:13). Perhaps he was ready to put his feet up and read the *Galilee Gazette*. But no! There was a crowd waiting for him!

Some disgruntled religious types had gathered to criticize his disciples' fasting habits. Along comes Jairus, a synagogue ruler with a daughter at death's door. Tired as he must have been, Jesus followed the man without hesitation and was nearly crushed by the crowd (Luke 8:42). When a woman with an incurable illness touched him, he healed her without even knowing who she was! And when he finally reached Jairus' house, he was greeted by obnoxious mourners who laughed at his faith. Still, Jesus was willing to have *more* power go out from him (Mark 5:30). There he performed one of his greatest miracles ever—raising a young girl from the dead! Clearly, Jesus was not just a servant—he was a *selfless servant*!

Many times, especially as leaders, we get so caught up with the "duties" of Christianity that we delegate opportunities to serve the weak and the lost. We have found we must emphasize that top leaders should still be meeting new people and bringing them to faith, because the more responsibility we have, the easier it becomes to "administer" rather than minister. Consistent delegation causes our hearts to harden. We lose our joy as we find ourselves just organizing and managing.

I remember a time when the ministry group I lead was growing rapidly, yet I had not personally met an unbeliever who became a disciple for years. The reason? I was not a *selfless servant* with the lost! After my repentance, I began to care for others much more. I brought more friends to church services than ever and enjoyed finding ways to help the poorer members of our congregation. When someone I met became a disciple, I didn't think, "Oh, good. Now I can say I was fruitful." Instead, I thought, "Why didn't I repent sooner?" If you aren't seeing "crowds" in your personal ministry, learn from Jesus' way with people and develop the heart of a *selfless* servant.

Tender Touches

Look at the thoughtful way that Jesus treated people. He knew that the woman's disease made her unclean under the law (Leviticus 15:19-27). He knew she was probably so ashamed of her condition that she couldn't even ask to be healed. After she touched his cloak, he could have let the woman leave anonymously, but he called attention to her just so that he could lift her up! Jesus spoke kindly and encouraged her. She never had to feel ashamed again. He was concerned about not only her sickness, but her emotions as well.

With Jairus' family Jesus also showed the depth of his concern and his attention to detail as he ordered them to give the girl food. Jesus was concerned that in their excitement over her resurrection, they might forget that she would be extremely hungry. (She had her life and *appetite* restored.) Jesus loved the people he was serving, and cared for their needs as individuals. These are just the kinds of things that can get lost in our urgency to teach and baptize. Eventually this lack of love can discourage those who would join our number and even gives reason for some to leave during the hard times.

Forceful Faith

Jesus had forceful faith and expected it of others: 1) The sickly woman struggled through a mob to touch him, yet she was healed, not because of her great effort but because of her great faith. 2) Jesus followed Jairus immediately, not because of Jairus' stress level, burden or frustration, but because he had forceful and persuasive faith.

Jesus' reaction to those without faith is just as noticeable: Jesus *ignored* those bringing the news that Jairus' daughter was dead (Mark 5:36). The scornful mourners got "worse" treatment—Mark says that he "put them all out" (Mark 5:40).

Do you have forceful faith? A friend of mine taught me to make up a list of "Five Impossible Things," and then pray for them every day. Try it yourself with forceful faith!

We see Jesus' selfless servant heart, his tender touches and his forceful faith. If we imitate his way with people, we, too, will see the crowds!

LIFE APPLICATION

1. Read through the following opportunities for serving selflessly everyday. Which of these convict you the most? Tell a close friend what you plan to do about it.
   - Leave work ready to meet and give to other disciples.
   - Study the Bible with an unbeliever, especially after having a "rough" day.
   - Take food to or visit someone hurting when you really don't have time.
   - Answer the phone when you planned to go to be early.
   - Reach out to someone while on your way to another appointment.
   - Listen to your spouse instead of listening to a CD.
   - Spend time talking with your kids instead of having them watch the Disney video.
   - Do follow-up calls instead of watching the news.

2. How encouraging are you really? Would people say that you are more free with positive or negative words?

3. Ask the people who know you best, including some non-Christians, to give you a rating on your sensitivity. Ask how you could improve and for some examples of how you've "blown it."

4. Are you seeing miracles in your life, or are you more like those whose remarks Jesus ignored? Is Jesus "going with you" because of your forceful faith, or does he get so bored with your prayers and attitude that he feels like asking you to leave?

·18·
Seeing and Not Seeing
Simon the Pharisee and the Sinful Woman

DIANE BROWN
Quito, Ecuador

Read Luke 7:36-50

> Then he turned toward the woman and said to Simon, "Do you see this woman? I came into your house. You did not give me any water for my feet, but she wet my feet with her tears and wiped them with her hair. You did not give me a kiss, but this woman, from the time I entered, has not stopped kissing my feet. You did not put oil on my head, but she has poured perfume on my feet. Therefore, I tell you, her many sins have been forgiven—for she loved much. But he who has been forgiven little loves little."
>
> Luke 7:44-47

Sugar ants! These minuscule creatures, barely visible to the naked eye, had decided to wreck havoc on my kitchen! I sprayed, I put out pellets, I finally called pest control. The following morning I stumbled into the kitchen only to find the persistent varmints marching in a steady line, laying siege once again to my kitchen counters. I sat dejectedly on the kitchen stool and surrendered to their goings on for a while.

They weren't even aware of my existence. As far as they were concerned, the place belonged to them. They just kept on going about their business, doing their little ant thing, heedless of the judgment being rendered on them at that very moment.

How like those little ants we lowly mortals are.

Jesus said to Simon, "Do you see this woman?"

Jesus might have said, *"What do you see, Simon, when you see this woman? Do you really see her? Or do you only see the gaudy attire and the loosened hair that broadcast her occupation to everyone in the city? Do you only see the filth of weeks spent on the dusty streets and the stench that not even an alabaster vial of perfume can mask? Do you see an ignorant, uncouth intruder, making a fiasco of this gathering?"*

"Simon, I have something to tell you." Jesus is able to cut through the muck and mire of cultural stigma, prejudice, gossip and critical judgments—right to the heart. His outspoken clarity (Luke 7:40) contrasted the Pharisee's hidden musings (7:39). Jesus' directness certainly exposed Simon's attempt to downplay his unspoken judgments against not only the sinful woman, but Jesus himself (7:39). Although claiming to be a spiritual leader, in truth Simon saw neither the woman nor himself—and certainly not Jesus—from a spiritual perspective.

Jesus did see the woman. Rather than being repulsed by her squalor, he was drawn to the purity of her heart. Her sin was as obvious as her brokenness. Jesus chose to honor her brokenness. The evidence of her garish life was undeniable, yet Jesus saw only the responses of a heart prompted by faith and overflowing with love.

Jesus' words should have cut Simon deeply: "But he who has been forgiven little loves little."

"Look again, Simon," he seems to say. *"Look deeper. Look beyond. You may see yourself. Look again, Simon, and you may just see God."*

Jesus Sees God

I can still remember the day that I first saw God.

I was reading a magazine article about space. According to the article, a satellite had been launched whose destiny was the outer reaches of the galaxy. It had been hurtling into space at mind-boggling velocity for a number of years, but had only covered half the distance. And that's as far as I ever got.

I couldn't believe what I was reading! This satellite had already been traveling for several years and had only gone half the distance! The finest, most technologically advanced machinery that the brightest, most well-trained minds could invent had traveled for years into space and had only gone half the distance. Even with my limited knowledge of astronomy, I was aware that we haven't begun to define the outer limits of the universe. (I had watched *Star Trek* after all!) I remember a feeling of awe as the enormity of all this set in. God had created this vast expanse I was reading about. He spoke and it came into being. But the most incredible thought of all was that out of the 5.5 billion people on the face of the earth, he has sought out me! He has a plan for me. He wants a relationship with me!

That God wants to have a relationship with me must be analogous to me wanting to have a relationship with...maybe an ant? The whole idea is just so ludicrous! Try to think of having a relationship with an ant—talking with it, caring for it, especially *dying* for it. It's so unfathomable! Yet I *know* that God has cared for me and protected me so many times in my life. As incredible as it seems, it is true—God sees me and cares for me. He loves me and wants to have a relationship with me.

John 1:18 says, "No one has ever seen God, but God the One and Only, who is at the Father's side, has made him known." Jesus knows God. Because of that knowledge, not a hint of self-doubt spills from him. Jesus' crystal clear view of God permeates every interchange with the Pharisee. Simon was mired down in the mud of his own sense of reality. He couldn't see himself. He couldn't see others. Tragically, he couldn't see Jesus. But Jesus had made God known to the brokenhearted woman. She saw herself. She was freed of all pretense and shared the crystal clear perspective on her place before God that Jesus had shown her. Her actions came from her new sense of reality. Once she saw Jesus, she responded the only way she could have—she was compelled to love (2 Corinthians 5:14).

How many times did Jesus change people's view of God and spirituality? How many times did he cause people who felt excluded to believe "I can follow a man like this"? Our world is full of people who need a new view of God and a new view of themselves. Our lives can help them find what they need the most.

LIFE APPLICATION

1. Who are you most like: Simon or the sinful woman? Choose one and explain.

2. What could pressure you to act like the Pharisees? What your peers think? What's socially or politically correct?

3. When are we, in the church, most like Pharisees today? Do you think it could never happen to us?

4. What do you think but never verbalize? Simon had quiet reservations, but Jesus was always forthright.

5. What do you do to make people who have been told they are unacceptable (or who feel unacceptable) feel loved and respected?

·19·
Give or Take?
Matthew, the Tax Collector

JOHN BRINGARDNER
Orlando, Florida

> As Jesus went on from there, he saw a man named Matthew sitting at the tax collector's booth. "Follow me," he told him, and Matthew got up and followed him.
> While Jesus was having dinner at Matthew's house, many tax collectors and "sinners" came and ate with him and his disciples. When the Pharisees saw this, they asked his disciples, "Why does your teacher eat with tax collectors and 'sinners'?"
>
> Matthew 9:9-11

"Another day, another denarius. Gotta hit the road, beat the streets and make a buck. Gotta move and groove; gotta shake and bake. There's gold in them there huts."

You've seen him before. You despise him. He's a hustler. Always has a gig to sell you. "Gonna make you rich." Just pony up a few dollars, and he'll get back to you. "Gotta hot stock." If you don't buy now, you'll miss out on a killing. "This case is worth a fortune." Just sign on the line, and you will be walking down easy street.

The world, it seems, is divided into givers and takers. We usually feel as though we are the givers and everyone else is a taker. We draw back. We become cynical. Wary. Weary. Wanting. We want the fast buck, the easy way, the comfortable life. Slowly, surely, the world squeezes us into its sinful mold. Before long we are all alone, fighting for our survival. We cling to our possessions, to our rights, to our feelings. We've stopped giving. We've become takers. Takers and keepers. Takers and users. Takers and abusers. We would never admit it. Many of us don't even see it.

Matthew, the Tax Collector

We surely don't want it. How did we get this way? Another day, another denarius.

Jesus met a man named Matthew. He was a taker. A tax taker. It's easy to judge a man like Matthew. How could he do it? How could he plunder his own people? How could he support such a corrupt government? Had he no conscience? But, I know how he feels. I've been there before, and so have you! Matthew was no different than us. He probably had a family with mouths to feed and clothes to buy. The kids needed new school scrolls. It was a good job, and somebody had to do it. So what if he had to miss a few church services every now and then? So what if he had to cut back on his contribution one month? God knew his heart. He would make it up...someday.

Well, "someday" actually came for Matthew. *He was sitting there at the office. It was tax season. Lots of work to do. Lots of sheep to fleece. Then it happened. This man began to speak. Some stopped to listen, then, others joined them. His customers began to leave. At first he thought of the lost business and cursed. Then a word caught his sharp ears and his interest. "I have come that you may have life. Life to the full."*

He left the office himself and crept a little closer toward the crowd.

"You must deny yourself, take up your cross and follow me."

Why? Where are you going?

"It is more blessed to give than to receive."

Preposterous!

But still the people, including Matthew, were listening. He was caught up in this man's words. This Jesus spoke to his heart. Jesus was honest and real—so different from the other teachers of the law. He finished speaking and the people cheered. They sang songs. Some wept. Others embraced. Then it happened. Jesus walked right on up to Matthew and said, "Follow me."

Matthew leapt...and left everything. You see, "someday" came. Somehow, Jesus got through. And Matthew would never be the same again.

Jesus gave Levi a new life, a new purpose, and perhaps even a new name. Comparing the gospels, it appears he was once known as "Levi." But no longer would he be *Levi*, from the Hebrew meaning "a joiner." Now he would be called "Matthew" from the Hebrew *Matteniah* meaning "a gift from God." Isn't that how God works? He takes us takers who want to be joiners and makes us givers by giving us the greatest gift we could ever know. He gives us eternal life. Levi's life changed forever. He had a gift from God. He was no longer a joiner or a taker, but a giver. The first thing Matthew did was to give a party. He invited all of his friends, family and associates and held a "sinner's dinner." And all those takers and "would-be" joiners came. Jesus was there and probably spoke as well. Who knows how many went home with a new name!

The question becomes: How could Jesus do it? How could he take this self-seeking traitor and turn him into a loyal, loving giver? The key is found in Mark 2:17: "On hearing this, Jesus said to them, 'It is not the healthy who need a doctor, but the sick. I have not come to call the righteous, but sinners.'" Jesus never forgot that all of us, no matter how we look on the outside, are sinners. We are sick people in need of a doctor. Too often, we look at some people, like Levi, and easily get intimidated. Jesus knew that Levi was "a mess in the flesh." He also knew what Levi could become with God.

When we lived in Los Angeles, my wife and I began studying the Bible with a couple from our neighborhood. The husband was about to become a partner in a major law firm in L.A., and I was a bit intimidated. We first met at a dinner party, and I felt the husband was not the least bit open. He hardly said a word the whole evening. I did not think he wanted to be there. (Later, I learned that he was suffering from the flu and pushed through so he could come to the party. Was I convicted!) His wife began attending our church, but I was convinced he was not interested. I knew all about his schedule and the travel and the long hours that would get in the way. In spite of my "great faith," he agreed to study the Bible and loved it! After studying the Bible, he was baptized into Christ, and two weeks later he baptized his wife. Quickly, they became some of our best friends. They truly were "a gift from God."

We need to look at people as Jesus did. We need to see people as they really are, yet believe in what they can become. We must fight through our feelings of doubt or intimidation and become givers of the gift of life. Then, our friends, family, acquaintances and associates can truly become "a gift from God."

LIFE APPLICATION

1. Is there someone in your life you can share with but haven't because you don't think they're open? Write down their names and begin praying for an opportunity to invite them to church or to study the Bible.

2. When was the last time you had a "sinner's dinner" and invited your friends and family over for a meal and message about Christ? Be bold and plan a "sinner's dinner" at your earliest opportunity.

3. Have you found yourself being a slave to comfort? How many hours of television are you watching? Do you hide in a book or in front of the computer? Make a pledge to unplug the "tube" for a week and spend time with friends, family or other disciples. See if it really is "more blessed to give than to receive."

·20·
Perceiving Potential
The Apostle Peter

BRIAN HOMET
Herndon, Virginia

> Jesus looked at him and said, "You are Simon son of John. You will be called Cephas."
>
> John 1:42b

What a strange introduction it was. Andrew came running into the house with the news that he had seen the Messiah. Then the two of them set off together so that Simon could meet him too. Now usually when you meet someone for the first time, you introduce yourself. With Jesus, Peter discovered that this was not necessary. Jesus already knew him.

Peter would learn to expect the extraordinary from Jesus soon enough, but on this their first encounter he must have been taken aback by him. "You are Simon son of John. You will be called Cephas." Instead of Jesus presenting himself, he introduced Peter! Not only did Jesus know Simon's name, he changed it! The name that his parents had given their baby boy, the name he had known and been known by all his life would no longer do. That day he would have a new name. That day he would begin a new life.

Simon to Peter

Simon was a fisherman. Jesus made Peter into a fisher of men. Simon was a very ordinary man living a very ordinary life. Jesus sent Peter to preach the life-changing gospel to all nations. Simon held a much worn, smelly fishing net. Jesus gave Peter the keys to the kingdom of God. Simon didn't think his life would have much impact beyond the shores of the Sea of Galilee. Peter helped to turn the world upside down, thanks to the man from

Galilee. What could possibly change the life of a man so radically? Not what, but who? Jesus.

Jesus looked at the world differently. Jesus looked at people differently. Those who knew Simon saw a fisherman and a friend. Jesus saw a future evangelist who would set the world on fire. Others saw volatility; Jesus saw passion. Others saw stubbornness; Jesus saw determination. Others saw Simon; Jesus saw Peter. Everybody knows that Jesus had an incredible faith in God. But in his relationship with Peter, we can see the faith he had in his disciples. Jesus could move mountains with his faith in God, yet what moved Peter was that Jesus believed in him! No, Simon isn't your name anymore; from now on you are Peter, *the rock*.

Jesus was nobody's fool. He knew what was in the hearts of men. He knew who Peter was...but he also knew who Peter could be. There were times that it seemed certain that he would fail, that he had failed. But Jesus never gave up on him, and Peter eventually became one of the leading figures in the movement of God!

Jesus' Vision

When I was baptized into Christ twenty-eight years ago by my friend John McGuirk in Paris, I made two decisions. First, I would follow my Lord Jesus no matter what the cost. Second, if it were God's will, I would go into the full-time ministry. That was my heart, although I had no idea what that meant. I learned later that while we were studying the Bible together, John had shared about me on the phone with his sister who was a ministry staff member with the church in Boston. At a meeting there she shared about me, and a prayer was offered — not just that I would become a Christian but that I would become an evangelist in the kingdom of God! Now that's vision!

Six months later I had the opportunity to be in a discipleship group led by a lead evangelist for the church. He told me time and again how he was praying for me. I don't remember too much from the sermons he preached twenty-seven years ago, but I have never forgotten that he was praying for me!

The prayers were answered, and I entered the full-time ministry; that is also when many challenges began. The main problem was that I had about as much spiritual ambition as a wet sock. I wanted to work full time for the Lord—no problem there—but that was it. As a young intern in the Harvard campus ministry, I never thought I would actually lead a campus some day, not to mention a church. I just never thought I could do it. I remember talking with other campus interns, guys who had aspired to more leadership, and I felt a pit of emptiness and fear inside me. I had no problems risking my body—I had done things like skydiving, rock climbing and white-water kayaking—but I had a huge problem with risking my heart. I had built walls to protect myself from hurt and disappointment. These same walls prevented me from believing that I would ever be able to do great things for God. I needed someone else to believe in me. I was a Simon who needed a new identity.

But God had more men ready to come into my life, men who looked at people differently, through the eyes of Jesus. Because of their faith in God, but also their faith in me, my wife and I have seen some amazing things happen for God. We started the church in Bucharest, Romania, and were given the opportunity to evangelize a portion of Eastern Europe from the Budapest church, where we were leading. A new life and vision—that's what Jesus is all about! "You are Simon...you will be called Cephas."

Peter found in Jesus a man who had a radical faith in God and in him. Jesus defied conventional thinking by believing that people can indeed change if someone gets in there and shows them the way. That's what he did with Peter. And with me. And he will do it with you, if you'll let him!

LIFE APPLICATION

1. In your own words, what have you learned about Jesus from his relationship with Peter?

2. What name might Jesus give you? How can trusting Jesus help you to turn your weaknesses into strengths?

3. How do you look at the people whom God has put into your life? Do you see only who they are now or who they can become? How much do you express your vision and your dreams for them?

·21·
The Disciple Whom Jesus Love
The Apostle John

STEVE BROWN
Quito, Ecuador

> Near the cross of Jesus stood his mother, his mother's sister, Mary the wife of Clopas, and Mary Magdalene. When Jesus saw his mother there, and the disciple whom he loved standing nearby, he said to his mother, "Dear woman, here is your son," and to the disciple, "Here is your mother." From that time on, this disciple took her into his home.
>
> John 19:25-27

You might expect it. If God were to walk the earth as a man, he would do everything excellently—"perfectly" you might say. And when it comes to friendship, Jesus again sets the standard. He shows us how to be a great friend.

As I studied the relationship between Jesus and John, I was challenged and convicted. I have been forced to examine and evaluate all my friendships: with my wife, kids and close friends in the church in Dallas where I serve as an elder. I have plenty of excuses: transition, turmoil, lack of time, pressure. But in view of Jesus' relationship with John, I need to change.

Realness

Jesus knew John. He saw his weaknesses, gave him the nickname "Son of Thunder," yet accepted him as he was (Mark 3:17). He did not hesitate to call him to be a follower (Mark 1:19-20) or to name him an apostle, in spite of his temperament. But while Jesus loved and accepted him, he still expected John to change. He rebuked him for wanting to roast a Samaritan village (Luke 9:51-56). He questioned his commitment and redirected his ambition for power when he and James came seeking the top positions in the kingdom (Mark 10:35-37).

Jesus was straightforward and direct. There was no pretense. He said what needed to be said. The incredible thing about John is that it would seem that he never doubted Jesus' love. In fact, when he wrote his gospel, he referred to himself as "the disciple that Jesus loved" five times! (John 13:23; 19:26; 20:2; 21:7, 20). What an incredible testimony to Jesus' friendship! Jesus was real. He was tough. But as he called John higher, his love for John was never in question.

We understand this in our relationships with our kids. Many years ago my son Marcos came home with a note for me:

> *My Dad is the bestest Dad in the hol wid worle and I love my Dad.*

I'm sure your sons will try to dethrone my newly acquired title, but the point is that Marcos believes this. There's no pretense. He's straightforward and direct. Even though we've had some hard moments, my relationship with Marcos remains tight!

Closeness

Knowing that ultimately he would have to face the cross alone, it would have been so easy for Jesus to maintain his distance—to keep people at arm's length. But he didn't. He threw himself into life completely. He included John again and again in the intimate and important events of his life and ministry. Closeness requires spending time together in a variety of situations. Jesus was the initiator. He wanted to be with John and wanted John to be with him.

This closeness is powerfully seen in John 13:23-26. At the Last Supper, John is seated at Jesus' left—closest to Jesus' heart. When he leans back and asks Jesus about the identity of the betrayer, Jesus confides in him, seemingly without the other apostles being aware of the significance of this interaction.

Openness

Jesus opened his heart to his friends. He didn't allow his position to deter him from letting them—especially John—know how he felt and what he struggled with. That may be why John knew how troubled Jesus was that night (John 13:21).

Of course, a few hours later in the garden, Jesus completely bared his very soul to his three closest friends. He told them: "My soul is overwhelmed with sorrow to the point of death. Stay here and keep watch with me" (Matthew 26:38). Jesus didn't retreat to be alone with his Father even then. He drew John and the others close to him. He opened his heart and shared his deepest feelings and struggles with them so they could really see him and be with him, all the while knowing that they were unworthy of his trust and confidence and would even fall asleep when he needed them the most.

Trusting

An even more stirring passage, however, is our theme scripture (John 19:25-27) where Jesus, the Son of God, is dying on the cross for the sins of all mankind. In his torment, he sees the need of his mother and he entrusts her to John's care. Even in this moment, Jesus goes beyond his suffering, beyond who he is and what he is doing, to let John know that he trusts him and needs him to take care of his mother. How challenging! He was God in the flesh yet he expressed *his* need for John's help and his confidence in John's ability to meet the need.

The relationship that Jesus had with John made a difference—it changed John's life. The "son of thunder" who once was ready to call down fire because of an irritation was so transformed that he became known as the Apostle of Love. In John's letters we see how deeply the ideas of love and loving one another permeated his writings. He was forever different because of his relationship with Jesus.

It is John who teaches us that our relationships with others reflect our relationship with God (1 John 4:19-20). To say that we love God when we don't love our brother, according to John, is a downright lie. For me, studying Jesus and John's relationship has forced me to reevaluate my own relationship with God.

When there is a problem with feeling real or close, or not trusting, I must remember the problem lies with me—not God. Then it's time to rebuild and renew my friendship with God. Time to take some prayer walks. Time to write things down. Time to revive hopes and dreams. And time to just talk and walk with my best friend—God.

LIFE APPLICATION

1. How real, close, open and trusting are your relationships with people? How real, close, open and trusting is your relationship with God?

2. What things do you struggle to entrust to God?

3. What do your relationships with people tell you you about your relationship with God?

·22·
Selection and Delegation
The Seventy-Two

ANDREW FLEMING
Moscow, Russia

> After this the Lord appointed seventy-two others and sent them two by two ahead of him to every town and place where he was about to go. He told them, "The harvest is plentiful, but the workers are few. Ask the Lord of the harvest, therefore, to send out workers into his harvest field."
> ...The seventy-two returned with joy and said, "Lord, even the demons submit to us in your name."
>
> Luke 10:1-2, 17

The ministry of Jesus was prefaced by the voice of one calling in the desert: "Repent, for the kingdom of heaven is near" (Matthew 3:1). Jesus himself repeated this message, but added something by calling people to follow and imitate him—to becoming fishers of men. Jesus had many followers. Many we do not know by name—they were simply the "unnamed" crowd of disciples traveling with him (unnamed to us, but surely not to him). But through his personal selection and training, Jesus organized these much loved people into a functioning discipleship group that would be able to fulfill the mission with which God had entrusted him.

At a crucial moment in his ministry Jesus spent a whole night praying, and after he had returned to the disciples he designated twelve to be "apostles" and later sent them to preach. No specific background information is included in the gospel accounts about them other than the names of their fathers or their professions. Who these disciples had been before their conversions was not all that significant what really mattered was that Jesus had chosen them to become part of "the Twelve."

Hands-On Training

From this point forward Jesus invested a great amount of time in personally training the Twelve. They closely observed him as he traveled around the countryside, teaching the crowds, encouraging faith in God and performing miracles. Their first test came in Luke 9 when Jesus decided to send them out two by two to preach the "good news" to the villages. This multiplication of "preachers" made such a great impact on people that even King Herod took notice and wanted to see Jesus.

The Twelve's safe return and positive report marked the beginning of an important change in the focus of the teaching of Jesus—he began to prepare the apostles for his predicted suffering and departure, in addition to training them for the mission. Ministry success exposed their hearts, and the apostles began to argue among themselves about who was the greatest. At times they were threatened by others who did powerful deeds in the name of Jesus, and at other times they wanted to immediately destroy those who refused the preaching of Jesus. Their self-focus, self-righteousness and sense of self-importance were completely wrong. Jesus redirected their attention to help them see the greatest challenge that lay ahead—to make more disciples. Crucial to their training was the understanding that what Jesus taught them must also be taught to reliable men who would in turn teach others.

In Luke 10 we read of another group of disciples whom Jesus handpicked and sent out: the "seventy-two" (some manuscripts say "seventy"). Many suggestions have been made as to the reason for these numbers, but Scripture does not give us a definitive answer.

Regardless of the rationale behind the number, Jesus selected this group and gave them the same commission that he had already given the Twelve—to go and preach the good news, "The kingdom of God is near." In the presence of the Twelve, Jesus emphasized the attitude of peace that they needed to have as his ambassadors—that their purpose was not to judge and condemn, but to warn and save. Jesus was able to test the quality of each pair's work (as well as demonstrate "accountability" to the Twelve), since his plan was to immediately visit each of the villages where he had sent the "seventy-two."

Satan Felt the Impact

The preaching of the Twelve may have gotten the attention of King Herod, but when the seventy-two began preaching the good news, Jesus said that he saw Satan fall like lightning from heaven. This could either be understood as a prophecy of Satan's impending expulsion from heaven, or simply as the fact that the devil was in shock when he heard the demons screaming and angels singing praises to God—seventy-two more had began to share this ministry of healing the sick, driving out evil spirits and preaching the "good news" of the kingdom. Jesus himself was full of joy as the Spirit allowed him to share in the Father's good pleasure—that which had been hidden from the wise and learned and had been revealed to little children. The hearts of prophets and kings had longed to see the coming of the kingdom of God— we are incredibly blessed to be able to see what we see and hear what we hear.

With the successful commissioning of the "seventy-two," Jesus apparently completed a phase of his ministry—selection. Jesus spent the remainder of his ministry strengthening his relationships with these disciples and completing their preparation and training. In the remaining narrative of the gospels there is no further mention of the "seventy-two" but in Acts 1:15 there is a new group: the "one hundred and twenty." This group was waiting for the promised Holy Spirit and most likely included the Eleven, the women who had traveled with Jesus, and the seventy-two. It would appear that the first church planting was completely handpicked by Jesus—not just the leaders, but even the team.

Jesus left nothing to chance—he chose the seventy-two because they were needed to form a leadership base on which his church and kingdom would be built and would fulfill the plan of God in preaching the "good news" to all nations. And Jesus is still looking for a few good men and women!

LIFE APPLICATION

1. In your discipling of others have you realized the importance of selection—a commitment to the teaching and training of another disciple of Jesus Christ?

2. Jesus viewed his disciples as being entrusted to him by God. Who are you caring for in the kingdom? How would things change if you thought more about the fact that those people are God's people and he has entrusted them to you to care for and nurture?

3. Does the consistency of your joy show that it is based on your personal success or on your salvation?

4. If Jesus today were picking a new "Twelve" or a new "seventy-two," list three reasons why you think he would give serious consideration to you.

·23·
Hard Heads, Hard Hearts
The Pharisees

BRIAN FELUSHKO
Vancouver, British Columbia, Canada

"Woe to you, teachers of the law and Pharisees, you hypocrites! You clean the outside of the cup and dish, but inside they are full of greed and self-indulgence. Blind Pharisee! First clean the inside of the cup and dish, and then the outside also will be clean."
Matthew 23:25-26

For anyone who has ever read the gospels at all, "Pharisee" brings to mind thoughts of the most hardhearted, closed-minded, self-righteous and outwardly religious people possible. While not every Pharisee would have fit this mold, this seems a fair description of the group's overall character. The gospel accounts are filled with references to these "blind guides." Have you ever wondered why? Do you silently pray, "God, I thank you that I am not like other men—robbers, evildoers, adulterers—or even like these Pharisees!" (See Luke 18:9-14). For years that is exactly how I reacted, all the while blind to my own self-righteousness and hypocrisy. When I was studying the Bible to become a disciple, it wasn't until my heart finally heard Jesus say to me "Woe to you…you hypocrites" that I saw myself as "the worst of sinners," and I repented.

We shouldn't imitate the heartless religious Pharisees, but we shouldn't avoid them either. On the contrary, Jesus' interactions with his most prideful and persistent detractors demonstrate a heart that each of us must capture, so that our righteousness will surpass that of the Pharisees and teachers of the law (Matthew 5:20).

A Heart Determined to Persevere

Nothing tests our determination like opposition. Through it, Satan is trying to discourage, dissuade, distract and divide. He knows that if he can get us to focus on the persecution or the persecutors, he has rendered us ineffective and unproductive. The Pharisees were Satan's chief servants in Jesus' life. They did everything possible to distract him from his mission and purpose. They doubted him, mocked him, questioned him, spied on him, confronted him, laid traps for him, falsely accused him, threatened him and joined forces with *their* opponents to plot against him. They harassed him at every turn.

Jesus, however, would not be distracted. He knew his purpose in this world was not to avoid pain, but to please God by finishing his work (John 4:34). On one occasion, the Pharisees came to him under the pretense of concern and warned him of Herod's intent to kill him. Jesus' reply demonstrates his unwillingness to yield to persecution: "I will reach my goal. In any case, I must keep going today and tomorrow and the next day" (Luke 13:32-33).

Satan will try to draw us away from doing God's work. God, however, has not called us to defend or protect ourselves. If we do that, we will only be working for ourselves—we will do nothing for God. Jesus, in his encounters with the Pharisees, demonstrates his steadfast determination and unfaltering zeal that enabled him to continue on and finish God's work.

A Heart Determined to Preach

Jesus did not avoid his persecutors; he confronted them. His was not an effort to defend himself, but to stand for God's word. Over and over again, he challenged their traditions and hypocrisy. He warned his disciples to beware of the "yeast" of the Pharisees (Luke 12:1); he challenged people to obey what they taught, but not to imitate their lives (Matthew 23:1-3); he spoke parables in their presence that were sure to offend (Matthew 15:12); and he gave them answers to their trick questions that left them silent (Matthew 21:23-27).

Why was Jesus so confrontational? He hated their sin—religious pride and arrogance. It angered him and left him "deeply distressed" (Mark 3:5). Jesus loved God and revered his Word. The Pharisees' absolute disregard for truth (though they styled themselves as great protectors of truth) left Jesus no choice but to speak out and expose their errors, lies and hypocrisy (Matthew 15:1-9; John 8:31ff). Their great influence over others left Jesus no choice but to confront them publicly, so that they would not lead truth-seekers astray. Not being distracted or intimidated by our persecutors does not always mean we just ignore them. Jesus' intensity in preaching the truth absolutely intensified the Pharisees' determination to oppose him. But like Jesus, we cannot back down to save ourselves; we must speak up to save others.

A Heart Determined to Love

When we read Matthew 23, Jesus' strongest and clearest denunciation of the Pharisees, what tone do we hear in his voice? Are these the rantings and ravings of a man who has been pushed over the edge, whose frustration level has reached its limit, who has finally had enough and who is going to have the last word before his enemies crucify him? Do we see in Matthew 23 a justification for harsh rebukes? No. In all his interactions with the Pharisees, Jesus' ultimate purpose was to save their souls. He was not trying to win an argument or put them in their place. He was trying to open their hearts and win them over to God.

Notice Jesus' lament in Matthew 23:37-39. We must never read the "seven woes" without understanding the context of love in which they were spoken. Jesus never gave up on the Pharisees. His last and strongest words were spoken to wake them up to the reality of their spiritual condition. As a "Pharisee" who was finally saved by these words, I am eternally grateful for Jesus' heart that was determined to persevere, preach and love. And I am determined to have that same heart so that more of the world's "Pharisees" can escape the deceit in which they live.

Jesus shows us that "Pharisees" must be, at times, exposed, at times challenged, and always loved with the unconditional love that God has for every soul. His strong words to people who felt they were the "true church" are a sharp reminder to us of how easy it is to cross the line from righteousness that honors God to self-righteousness that disgusts him. May God help us to stay humble servants, always grateful for grace and always open to correction.

LIFE APPLICATION

1. Do you have a heart determined to persevere in the face of ongoing persecution? Write down who is persecuting are you and how. How have you responded outwardly? In your heart? What specific things do you need to do to change?

2. Why did Jesus stand up and preach the truth even though it intensified the persecution he received? When you know you should speak but don't, what is the real problem? What must you focus on in order to have a heart that is determined to preach?

3. Jesus was never vindictive or vengeful in his rebuke and correction of the Pharisees. Do you *love* the "Pharisees" that are in your life and that you encounter? Jesus was not only a friend of tax collectors and sinners, but he was also a friend of Pharisees. Are you? What can you do today that will demonstrate such love?

· 24 ·
A Real Friend
Martha and Mary

TRICIA STATEN
Chicago, Illinois

"I tell you the truth," Jesus said to them, "no one who has left home or wife or brothers or parents or children for the sake of the kingdom of God will fail to receive many times as much in this age and, in the age to come, eternal life."

Luke 18:29-30

Jesus gave up his home, his job, his financial security, his family and ultimately, his life to seek and save the lost. During his travels with his disciples, Jesus found a place of refuge with a loving family in the little town of Bethany. His choice to spend time with them during the last weeks of his life is evidence of the closeness of their relationship. His friendship with Martha, Mary and their brother was intimate, compassionate and spiritually focused. It is important as well as encouraging to know that Jesus needed friends, just as we do. These sisters, however, were very different in their strengths and weaknesses, and Jesus responded to them according to their individual needs.

The Better Choice

Bethany was a city two miles east of Jerusalem. One time, as Jesus and his disciples were passing through the village, Martha "opened her home" to them (Luke 10:38). Her heart began in the right place, as she planned to serve a feast fit for a king. Her preparations were extensive, and she was convinced that she needed Mary by her side. Upon Jesus' arrival, Mary was drawn to his feet to listen. His words were powerful and captivating — they seemed to reach down into her very heart and grab hold of it. His words gave more hope and purpose to her life than she had known before. Martha's heart, though, became overwhelmed and burdened with the preparations for her special meal. She was convinced that Jesus would feel her burden as well.

Jesus didn't stop to correct Martha in her whirlwind of preparation. He was as accepting of her hospitality as he was of Mary's choice to listen. Jesus loved this family, each as individuals (John 11:5). In fact, his ease with them allowed Martha to go to him with her feelings unmasked. She was open for direction from the Master. "Lord, don't you care that my sister has left me to do the work myself? Tell her to help me!" Jesus recognized that she was worried and distressed over many things, yet he did not react to Martha's disrespect and demands with anger.

"Martha, Martha," began his compassionate response as he revealed to her the truth: Mary's choice was the right and lasting one. Jesus' love for his friends never caused him to be sentimental or to shade the truth so they would like him.

As appreciative as Jesus must have been for Martha's desire to serve him, what he wanted most to see from her was a single-minded desire to know him and to know his teachings. His desire remains the same for us today, and he loves us enough to correct us when we get off course, just as he corrected his good friend from Bethany. I, like Martha, need that correction when I get so wrapped up in preparing to serve people that I am too distracted and exhausted to serve them when they arrive for the evening.

Jesus Serves

Toward what would be the end of his ministry, Martha and Mary sent out a plea for Jesus to come heal their brother, Lazarus, who was near death. Jesus waited for two days before going to Bethany. Upon his arrival, Lazarus had been in the grave four days. The one who knew all things had certainly known that Lazarus would die, but he delayed his response to Martha and Mary's request for a reason. Jesus knew what would have the greatest impact on the faith of Martha, Mary, the Jews who had gathered to comfort them, and even us today. The miracle of healing a dying man was great, but to show the absolute love and unmatchable power of God in raising a man from the dead was even greater.

Jesus is always aware not only of our situation, but also of how it fits with the much larger picture. When we ask for Jesus' intercession, we can be assured that his will is carried out in our lives, although his will may not always fall in line with our requests or our timetables.

Jesus was faithful and compassionate in his response to his grief-stricken friends. "When Jesus saw her [Mary] weeping, and the Jews who had come along with her also weeping, he was deeply moved in spirit and troubled" (John 11:33). Jesus was not emotionally detached from people. He was not the distant figure many of us as children saw in stained-glass mosaics—so heavenly that he couldn't know us or really know what we felt. Rather, we see a man with complete empathy for those around him no matter what their struggles (Hebrews 2:18, 4:15).

Martha and Mary's final encounter with Jesus takes place six days before the Passover, during the last week before his crucifixion (see John 12:1ff). While Martha was serving at a dinner in his honor, Jesus was reclining at the table. With a sacrificial gesture, Mary served and honored Jesus by anointing him with perfume. Judas saw a waste of money, but Jesus saw her heart. Her love and vulnerability touched him deeply. He recognized that Mary was doing what she could for him—that along with the perfume, she was pouring out her love for him. Jesus measures our service by our surrender to him. He protects us and delights in us when we do all that we can. At the end of a similar story in Matthew 26, Jesus promised that the story of the woman's love would always be told whenever the gospel was preached. Our surrender will never go unnoticed by God (John 12:26), even if those around us are critical of how foolish our vulnerability seems.

In both the hospitality and the anointing accounts, we see a Jesus who looks not at the expense or at the amount of our service; he simply looks at the heart and the intent. And woven through both accounts of service is the deep friendship that he enjoyed with these down-to-earth women from Bethany. We must understand that we are to seek not only his will, but his friendship as well.

LIFE APPLICATION

1. Do you typically choose to learn from Jesus *before* the challenges of your day come?

2. When you pray, do you seek for God's will to be done in the stressful situations? If his will and your will differ, do you pray that he changes your heart to accept it?

3. Are you willing to appear foolish in your service to God?

4. How does it affect you to know that Jesus wants friendship with you, just as he wanted it with this family? What are you doing to nurture that friendship?

· 25 ·
Death Be Not Proud
Lazarus

G. STEVE KINNARD
Fair Lawn, New Jersey

> Jesus said to her, "I am the resurrection and the life. He who believes in me will live, even though he dies; and whoever lives and believes in me will never die. Do you believe this?"
>
> John 11:25-26

During his ministry Jesus confronted and overcame all the major problems of human life: illness, hunger, storms, demon possession, and even death. On several occasions he took those who had died and raised them back to life. This story is perhaps the most dramatic, and not only reveals his divine power, but the depth of his character.

Jesus Loved

We live in an age of great loneliness and isolation. Mother Teresa of Calcutta, upon visiting the United States, commented, "In the United States you have a poverty which is just as desperate as the poverty of India. It is the poverty of loneliness." In our cities people live behind locked doors staring out of peepholes, afraid to unlatch the security lock without presentation of proper identification. How many times have we read of the discovery of a deceased person due to the odor alerting others to the death?

To curb the tide of loneliness we find friends. But good friends were as hard to find in the first century as they are today. Jesus found some best friends in the household of Lazarus, Martha and Mary. It seems that every time Jesus was in the vicinity of Bethany, he stayed at their house. Many people probably clamored for this honor, but Jesus wanted to be in the home of those he knew and loved whenever he was in their region. With crowds following him everywhere demanding healings and miracle shows, Jesus probably felt acutely the need to be among people who loved him as a friend and not for what he could give to them, people who enjoyed his company and conversation, people who laughed at his jokes. Lazarus' clan was like family to him. We have all felt this need in our lives, so we should not be surprised that Jesus, being human, felt it, too.

Jesus Wept

Upon hearing about the death of his close friend Lazarus, Jesus wept. This is one of the Bible's greatest statements. It shows that Jesus really felt the emotions that we feel. He was fully divine and fully human at the same time. Because of this, he knows what it is like to experience loss, pain, hurt and fatigue. He can relate to everything we feel.

These two words in John 11:35 also give us a window into the heart of Jesus—he was not afraid to show his emotions. Why did he cry? Scripture does not say, but maybe he felt the hurt of Mary and Martha (the most likely explanation). Maybe he was expressing the hurt of the loss of his friend, Lazarus. Maybe he was anticipating his own death. The exact reason for his outpouring of emotion is unknown. We do know that he was not afraid to demonstrate how he felt.

I remember the first time I saw my dad cry. I must have been six or seven. He had received news that his favorite uncle, Uncle Herbert, was dying of cancer. He started praying for Uncle Herbert at the dinner table. During his prayer he starting making funny sounds. I thought he was laughing at some fond memory of his uncle. I started to laugh with him. Then I realized he was not laughing. He was crying. My father was man enough to cry in front of his family. I have always appreciated that about him. He showed a bit of Jesus to me that day.

Jesus Won

When Jesus first received the news about Lazarus' illness, he essentially declared, "This illness is not going to prove fatal" (John 11:4). It must have seemed to his disciples that Jesus was wrong. After all, when they arrived in Bethany, Lazarus was dead. They may have wondered, *Why did he wait around so long? Why didn't he rush to the scene? Maybe he really blew it this time.*

But Jesus did not blow it. He never does. He was in control of the situation from beginning to end. He always is. He knew he was the resurrection and the life. He went to the tomb of Lazarus and commanded him to come forth. I remember an old, country preacher once commenting that it was a good thing that Jesus called Lazarus by name because if he had just said, "Come forth!" then every corpse in the cemetery would have come to life.

The story of Jesus raising Lazarus from the dead foreshadows Jesus' own resurrection after three days in the tomb. Death could not and cannot hold Jesus. He is victor over death! To all of humanity, death is the unconquerable foe. The common phrase is "Two things are certain—death and taxes." Some may be able to evade the tax man (I'm certainly not advocating cheating on your taxes here!), but none of us can hide from the grim reaper! Only Jesus could conquer death. The story of the resurrection of Lazarus is preface to the greatest story ever told: Jesus rose on the third day. In rising, he beat death. Jesus won!

Jesus with Lazarus: Life confronts death and life wins. "'Where, O death, is your victory? Where, O death, is your sting?' …thanks be to God! He gives us the victory through our Lord Jesus Christ" (1 Corinthians 15:55-57). When Jesus brought his friend Lazarus out of that tomb and when he came out of his own tomb a few days later, he taught us that nothing, not even death, can separate us from the love of God.

LIFE APPLICATION

1. Who are your deepest relationships in the kingdom? Who would you like to be closer to?

2. What do you appreciate most about the love of Jesus?

3. Do you fear death? How does your relationship with Jesus change the way you once thought?

·26·
Entrusted and Transformed
Mary Magdalene

CARYN HOMET
Herndon, Virginia

> When Jesus rose early on the first day of the week, he appeared first to Mary Magdalene, out of whom he had driven seven demons. She went and told those who had been with him and who were mourning and weeping."
>
> Mark 16:9-10

As Mary stood outside the tomb, crying and perplexed, she barely turned to look at the "gardener" who spoke to her. But as soon as he uttered her name, "Mary," she recognized the voice that was so familiar to her (John 20:16). It was her Lord! It was Jesus! He was alive!

The past few days had been a nightmare for Mary. They had taken Jesus to crucify him. She had been there to see him nailed to a cross. She had seen the pain in his eyes, heard the agony of his final groans and watched his bleeding body as it hung limp and lifeless. Others had forsaken him, but Mary was loyal to the end. She and her companions had stayed at the foot of the cross until Jesus breathed his last. Even as they went to the tomb to anoint his body, they were there for the one who had always been there for them. She did all she could to express her love and loyalty to him, for it was his love that had rescued her, and she would never forget it.

When Mary first met Jesus, she was wrought with seven demons. They were controlling her mind and body and preventing her from guiding her own actions and thoughts. One demon is enough, but Mary had seven. And Jesus, in a single moment, cast them all out of her. He had healed her and set her free.

Accepted and Befriended

But Jesus' love didn't end there. Others whom Jesus had healed went their separate ways. Some wanted to stay with him, but it was not in Jesus' plan. He let Mary Magdalene remain with him and be a part of those closest to him. Although it was twelve men who were the focus of Jesus' ministry and discipling, the significance of the women in his group was not to be overlooked. In a day and age when women were not considered "important," Jesus highly regarded and valued the women who had dedicated themselves to him. It is evident through the gospels that Mary, through her service and her friendship, was a vital part of Jesus' life and ministry.

Jesus was not only *her* friend, he considered her *his* friend. Her troubled past didn't matter. He saw her not simply as "the woman who had been demon-possessed," but as his friend, Mary. What a privilege and joy it must have been for her to walk with Jesus, to be his friend and to feel his acceptance!

Disciples of Jesus today have that same opportunity. Through Christ we are healed, accepted and called his friend (John 15:15). Yet, it's easy to let some "demons" from our past creep back into our lives—the demons of deceit, selfishness, worldliness, pride and insecurity. In becoming a disciple twelve years ago, I was motivated by the love and acceptance of Jesus. As the only one who truly knew me, and yet still loved me, I felt so grateful to him.

However, as a young Christian, it was difficult for me to open up to others about what was going on inside of me. I feared that my sin would make me unlovable, and as a result, I built a protective wall of pride around me. Inside I was extremely insecure, but I overcompensated by being prideful, cold and aloof. The thought, *If they really knew me, they wouldn't love me* resounded in my heart, paralyzing me.

But God is patient and through the love and acceptance of some persistent disciples, the wall began to crumble. I found that as I opened up and let people inside, the very opposite of what

I had feared happend: I actually became more lovable to those around me! Like Mary, I was able to *feel* the acceptance of Jesus.

Entrusted with the Gospel

What an honor it must have been to be the first witness of the greatest victory of all time—the resurrection! Jesus had blessed Mary's loyalty by choosing her to be the first bearer of the "good news." Jesus had healed her. He had accepted her. Now he had rewarded and honored her with the incredible gospel message, "Jesus is risen!"

How honored I feel to be entrusted with the same message 2,000 years later! It's still just as true as it was the day Mary witnessed it. And Jesus' love for me is just as strong as it was for Mary Magdalene. He knows all my sin, but sees me as his friend, Caryn. At the time, God had entrusted me with bringing the gospel first to Romania, and then to Hungary and to all of Eastern Europe. The demons were attacking, but the purpose with which God had entrusted me kept the demons from getting back in. I want to leave no arid places that would give Satan an opportunity to regain control of my life (Matthew 12:43-45). Because of Jesus' friendship with me, I, like Mary Magdalene, want to remain loyal to him to the end.

God seems to delight in entrusting his truth and power to unlikely people. Mary's is one more amazing story of how God took someone from under Satan's control and turned her into a vessel to carry treasure. Let us allow Jesus' vision for our lives to motivate us to share the good news with others around us.

LIFE APPLICATION

1. What are some of the "demons" that Jesus has cast out of you? Have you let some of them creep back in? What do you need to do to get rid of them again?

2. Do you open up freely to those God has put in your life, or do you let fear stop you? Who can you talk to today about your decisions?

3. How faithful are you with the message that Jesus has entrusted to you? What practical decision do you need to make to be more active in sharing your faith?

· 27 ·
Giving All She Had
The Widow at the Temple

PAT GEMPEL
Philadelphia, Pennsylvania

> Jesus sat down opposite the place where the offerings were put and watched the crowd putting their money into the temple treasury. Many rich people threw in large amounts. But a poor widow came and put in two very small copper coins, worth only a fraction of a penny.
> Calling his disciples to him, Jesus said, "I tell you the truth, this poor widow has put more into the treasury than all the others. They all gave out of their wealth; but she, out of her poverty, put in everything—all she had to live on."
>
> Mark 12:41-44

Living his last week on this earth in the shadow of the cross, Jesus had much to teach his disciples. As he sat with them at the temple, he watched the crowd putting their money into the treasury. He *watched* the giving, but he *saw* the hearts—of both rich and poor. The widow who gave two coins, all she had to live on, was the one he lifted up as an example to his disciples. In the same way that he watched these Jewish people giving their offering 2,000 years ago, so he watches us as we give…and so he sees our hearts. Are we just giving, or are we sacrificing? The one who gave all he had wants to teach us to give as this poor widow gave.

Financial Sacrifice

The widow's offering shows us that Jesus sees our heart and sacrifice. Without ever speaking to her, he made her gift the biblical standard for financial sacrifice. The widow gave *all she had to live on* (Luke 21:4). Being a poor widow, she likely had no income. She was probably hungry and surely without any financial hope. Yet, her faith in God was evident from her actions. The Bible doesn't tell us specifically what happened to her, but we can know that God took care of her needs (Matthew 6:25-34).

We remember special friends of ours, the Bairds, when they sold their home and contributed most of the money to help advance world missions. Jesus saw their example of financial sacrifice, too. The Bairds gave much and the widow gave little, yet in the eyes of the Lord, both gave sacrificially.

Emotional Sacrifice

Emotional sacrifice is challenging. Jesus mentions the sacrificial widow to his disciples then gives them this warning: "Be careful, or your hearts will be weighed down with dissipation, drunkenness and the anxieties of life, and that day will close on you unexpectedly like a trap" (Luke 21:34).

Sacrifice requires that we take control of the "anxieties of our lives." Unfortunately, emotional sacrifice cannot be made "once for all time." It is a daily struggle. My husband Bob's character is thoughtful, compassionate and loving, but also independent and withdrawn. He used to spend days at a time alone, working on complex physics problems. Every day Bob needs to make emotional sacrifices in order to change. Now, after twenty years he is hospitable, an experienced counselor, a godly teacher and an elder. He has changed so much that few who meet him realize what he was like before.

For me, totally different kinds of changes were needed. I am basically outgoing, hospitable and goal-oriented, but my emotional sacrifice was to overcome self-righteousness, anger and, indeed, fits of rage. These daily sacrifices, over time, have resulted in great victories.

In order to change character weaknesses like these, true emotional sacrifice is needed. First, we must admit that we are sinful. Second, we must realize Jesus has called us to follow him and be righteous. Third, we must humbly commit to change.

Fourth, we must change. The solutions are simple, the emotional sacrifice is not. The challenge is great, but the reward is greater. Today, Bob is even more hospitable than I am, and I have grown in self-control and have become more patient and loving. We are both committed to righteousness in these difficult emotional areas. Some days are better than others—but we offer our best to Jesus every day.

Physical Sacrifice

Physical sacrifice is central to our commitment to Jesus. The widow, giving all she had to live on, was certainly sacrificing physically. Jesus' dying on the cross is the apex of both emotional and physical sacrifice.

When I think of physical sacrifice, I think of Joyce Arthur. She is committed to being fit and trim. For some, weight control is easy, for others, it is more difficult. Unfortunately, Joyce has a tendency in the flesh towards being heavy, but you wouldn't know it, since Joyce lives by her tendency in the spirit—self-control!

Another great example is Renie Sebald, a deacon's wife in Philadelphia who was diagnosed with Chronic Fatigue Syndrome years ago. Renie needed to prioritize her life to meet important rather than urgent needs. She must constantly battle the anxiety and pressures of being a wife, being a mother of four, studying the Bible and helping counsel other disciples. Physically, priorities must be set, reexamined and set again. Renie is able to do this because she has God, her husband and other godly women advising her. She is able to accomplish as much as is physically possible for her. She may not accomplish as much as those more physically able, but she gives with all the energy she has—just like the widow.

God will help us discern what we can give physically, and God is capable of giving his strength when ours is failing. Paul learned to rely on the Lord through physical (and emotional) suffering (2 Corinthians 1:3-9). God's grace is sufficient. Each of us, with the help of God and our loving brothers and sisters, must live physically sacrificial lives daily (Philippians 2:12).

All Is All

The widow's financial, emotional and physical sacrifices were all a part of her spiritual sacrifice. Romans 12:1 reads,

> "Therefore, I urge you, brothers, in view of God's mercy, to offer your bodies as living sacrifices, holy and pleasing to God—this is your spiritual act of worship."

Jesus is eager to notice sacrifice in the lives of his followers. His life was spent day after day giving himself away to others for their good. He gave in every way, just as the widow did. And he longs to bless those who follow his—and her—example. He blesses because we give our all, not because we give the most.

LIFE APPLICATION

1. Make a list of people to whom you would give everything you own if they were in need.

2. Make a list of people for whom you would die today.

3. What holds you back from giving more than you do? How can you change?

4. Think of the ways you have sacrificed financially, emotionally, physically and spiritually. Now think of the ways God has blessed you in each of these areas.

· 28 ·
Political 'Principle'
Pontius Pilate

STEVE STATEN
Chicago, Illinois

> In the sight of God, who gives life to everything, and of Christ Jesus, who while testifying before Pontius Pilate made the good confession, I charge you to keep this command without spot or blame until the appear-ing of our Lord Jesus Christ...
>
> 1 Timothy 6:13-14

Paul's knowledge of what occurred between Jesus Christ and Pontius Pilate shows that this encounter had already become part of the consciousness of the Christian faith, most likely prior to the publishing of the Gospels. The encounter between Pilate and Jesus is also planted deep within the consciousness of people even today. During the seventies, I remember hearing a radio commentator announce the results of a survey concerning which historical figure people would most enjoy conversing with over dinner. Interestingly, two of the top three choices were Jesus Christ and Pontius Pilate.

Both Pilate and Jesus were in deep trouble when they met. In the case of Pilate, the Jewish historian Josephus recorded that Pilate's regime had caused a number of serious problems among the Jews. A flap over busts of the emperor that Jews considered idolatrous led to a showdown in which the Jews made it clear that they would die for their position. Pilate gave in.* In another incident, his soldiers slaughtered many Jews over a conflict involving an aqueduct construction. On another occasion, when Pilate probably meant to teach the Jews a lesson, he mixed the blood of some Jews with pagan sacrifices, further widening the chasm between him and his subjects (Luke 13:1-2). Pilate had enemies among his subjects. The governor was certainly in need of a political victory with the Jews.

Doing the Good We Ought To Do

Compared to the previous struggles, the "Jesus dilemma" made the governor's worries look minuscule. Jesus was a perfect Jew who had been charged with the most scandalous charges imaginable. He was accused of stirring up the people (Luke 23:5), being an insurrectionist (Luke 23:13-14), a blasphemer (Matthew 26:65), and a criminal (John 18:30). And as he stood before Pilate, alone and accused, his close friend had just betrayed him, another had denied him and all his other friends had cowered in fear and deserted him. Less than a week earlier, the masses had given homage and accolades to Jesus as he entered Jerusalem, and yet those same crowds were now asking for his death. Everything that Jesus had lived for appeared to be on the brink of being lost forever. His dearly loved disciples were also in danger from the mob reaction.

When we think of Jesus, we think of one who always did what was right. When we think of Pilate, we think of the one who knew what he ought to do and what he wanted to do, but did not do it. Recently a man was baptized into Christ where I lead the ministry. A few months later while we were talking, we realized that we had both lived in the same town at the same time. We then realized it was on the same side of town. We eventually discovered we shared the same alley and knew some of the same neighbors. Then a picture flashed in my mind, and I said, "John, did you have a shiny black Camaro?" He did, and as it turns out, he had lived directly behind me. We remembered meeting each other, but the reason that I recalled the fleeting "hello" from ten years earlier is that I remembered chickening out and not reaching out to him. This omission was carved in my memory. Jesus had no such memories. He always took every opportunity.

What Is Truth?

Treacherous Jews sought to destroy Jesus. Upon hearing the charges made by his fellow Jews in front of a Gentile, Jesus did "not even reply to a single charge—to the great amazement of the governor" (Matthew 27:14). Jesus' self-control stumped Pilate.

Later, in another conversation, Jesus told Pilate that he was a king and, "for this reason I came into the world, to testify to the truth" (John 18:37). This was audacious, yet it was the essential part of Jesus' confession since he was revealing his purpose in life. Pilate had never heard such things. Jesus then revealed his absolute position—"Everyone on the side of truth listens to me" (John 18:37). Poor Pilate. This gallant, ill-fated Jew was forcing him to face "truth" head on, when all he wanted to do was avoid another political blunder. He replied with the typical escapist response, "What is truth?"

I remember a situation that happened to me ten years ago when I was working as a systems analyst for a large company. I was on an elevator with a few people, including a vice-president, and he was telling a derogatory joke about Christ. I felt both angry and afraid at the same time. I wanted to say something, yet I felt the pressure of knowing who he was. I decided to wait until we got off the elevator and then respectfully told him that I did not appreciate the joke. We ended up talking for two and a half hours about Jesus, religion, philosophy and our personal lives. He eventually told me that I had the ideal values, but if I would adopt a relativist attitude, I would reach my potential in life. He had in essence said, like Pilate, "What is truth?" Yet, unsettling thoughts haunted him and nine months later he called me into his office to continue our discussion about the absolute truth. I knew that I had made an honest confession of the gospel earlier. Jesus remains as our perfect example of one who bore witness to God. We, as witnesses like him, must also answer the prevailing relativism with the absoluteness of the Gospel.

People-Pleasing Pilate

After having found Jesus innocent of the charges, three times Pilate "appealed to them," but in the end he surrendered Jesus to the will of the crowd who with loud shouts demanded that he be crucified (Luke 23:13-24). And their shouts prevailed. The Jews were ready to use this incident to get Pilate in trouble back in Rome (John 19:12). In these strenuous moments, Jesus still let Pilate know that he was guilty of sin (John 19:11). Instead of seeking an escape from his predicament, Jesus testified to the truth about God and tried to convict Pilate. Jesus was still preaching and reaching out to the lost—even his executor! Jesus had an impact on him with his confession and "from then on, Pilate tried to set Jesus free" (John 19:12). The governor was moved, but sadly not moved enough.

It is well known that Pilate succumbed to the pressure and released Jesus to the urging of the people. Jesus died for the truth, whereas Pilate embraced political expediency and purposefully avoided absolutes. Jesus died, but he lived again, and he lives today! Pilate lived (and kept his job—for a while), but his name was written in infamy.

In Jesus' encounter with Pilate, we see courage and integrity in stark contrast with political correctness. The world still has too many "Pilates." It needs more disciples of Jesus.

LIFE APPLICATION

1. How do you fare under negative chatter about *your* Christian convictions?

2. In the midst of high pressures, who do you relate to: Jesus or Pilate? Jesus was "sold out" to his Father's will and Pilate was "sold out" to public opinion.

3. Has a non-Christian ever been so inspired by your life that they attempted, even feebly, to defend your cause. Pilate tried at least three times to plead Jesus' case. Think about your family, neighbors and friends.

*Josephus, *Antiquities of the Jews,* Book 18, 3, 1-2.

·29·
Love Thy Enemy
Judas Iscariot

TAMMY FLEMING
Moscow, Russia

> So Jesus told him, "What you are about to do, do quickly."
> But no one at the meal understood why Jesus said this to him. Since Judas had charge of the money, some thought Jesus was telling him to buy what was needed for the festival, or to give something to the poor. As soon as Judas had taken the bread, he went out. And it was night.
> When he was gone, Jesus said, "Now the Son of Man is glorified and God is glorified in him.
> John 13:27b-31

Judas Iscariot. Traitor. One of the Twelve. Jesus was not naive or deceived when he included a thief in his inner circle. He knew all men (John 2:24-25), knew their thoughts (Matthew 12:25), knew absolutely that Judas would betray him to death (John 13:11). Jesus knew that he would spend three years loving him, training him and investing everything he had in him, along with the other Eleven. To what end? Wretchedness. Woe. Desperation. Destruction. Jesus himself foretold that the destiny of his betrayer would be so wretched it would have been better for him if he had never been born! (Matthew 26:24). Yet, Jesus himself selected him.

Devil in Disguise

What was it like for Jesus, living not only with the knowledge that he would soon die a horrible, violent death, but having to live daily with his mortal enemy? "Have I not chosen you, the Twelve? Yet one of you is a devil!" (John 6:70). A devil—sleeping under the same roof, sharing the same bread! Jesus not only tolerated him, but amazingly lavished love on him. The same love he showed the other Eleven, so perfect and so sincere that not one of the others even suspected Judas. Not even after three years together. No one suspected Judas as he helped himself regularly to the contents of the group's money bag (John 12:6). He was present at Jesus' private family get-togethers. He watched the miracle of the five loaves and the two fish. He received authority from Jesus himself to drive out demons and heal every disease and sickness.

Daily Unconditional Love

How is this possible? My own spirit squirms today as I doggedly try again to put myself in Jesus' place, to compare my heart to his. I know that Jesus was tempted in every way, just as I am, but was without sin (Hebrews 4:15). How could he put up with this monster in his face day after day? I would have rebelled. I would have tried to hurt him, to get revenge, to get rid of him. I would have hated him! How could Jesus love him?

One of the most constantly challenging aspects of my discipleship is learning to imitate Jesus' complete submission to God's will. Jesus trusted in God emotionally, no matter what it cost. He chose Judas so that the Scriptures, which God inspired, would be fulfilled (John 13:18). It meant he had to suffer emotionally every time he looked at Judas. I don't think Jesus ever got numb or indifferent to Judas. Quite to the contrary, he lived with his betrayer, and he loved him (John 13:1). The struggle was fresh every day, and just as poignant every day. Jesus must have taken that to God with loud cries and tears...every day! How Jesus' heart must have ached as he taught on the mountainside: "Do not give dogs what is sacred; do not throw your pearls to pigs. If you do, they may trample them under their feet, and then turn and tear you to pieces" (Matthew 7:6). Judas. "Be on your guard against men; they will hand you over to the local councils and flog you in their synagogues" (Matthew 10:17). Judas. "Brother will betray brother to death" (Matthew 10:21). Judas. "Love your enemies and pray for those who persecute you" (Matthew 5:44). Judas.

Decision to Love

As an American living in Moscow, I'm often amazed by the hidden pain and suffering in so many of the former Soviet people's lives. Last week, sitting with a group of friends on my living room floor, we talked about the times in our past when we've been afraid. My friend Marina from Uzbekistan related a story from her childhood when armed soldiers stormed her little town and school. She was the age my daughter is now, six, and in the first grade. Not sure she was out of danger herself, Marina peered out of an upper-story window as the attackers sprayed the school yard with bullets. Her best friend's class had been caught in the line of fire, and her eyes frantically searched the scene for some sign of her friend in her little white dress. She finally saw her, fallen among others who were strewn about the ground, a great red stain spreading over the white dress.

As I think about what it is like for Marina to decide to love the soldiers in her memory, I imagine what it was like for Jesus to love Judas. How could he love him? Because he revered his Father's plan and his Father's word. He denied himself and completely submitted to God. He didn't question God's plan. He didn't say, "This is too hard"—not at any point! "The scripture cannot be broken" was his deep conviction (John 10:35). Why could he choose to love Judas? "Jesus knew that the Father had put all things under his power, and that he had come from God and was returning to God..." (John 13:3). So at the hour prior to his betrayal, he got up and washed Judas' feet. "For the joy set before him [he] endured the cross" (Hebrews 12:2).

Jesus was unbelievably secure in God's love for him and certain of the goodness and perfection of every detail of God's plan (Romans 12:2). This simple trust empowered him to do what I find unfathomable! I know I don't forgive like Jesus. I know I don't give and love unconditionally like Jesus. I know I don't face my struggles head on and accept suffering like Jesus.

Because I don't trust God like Jesus, I set limits. I'm too tired to make another phone call. I can't think about moving to another city—we just moved into a new apartment! I tend to react to the Judases in my life emotionally, as if God were punishing me for something, instead of embracing them as part of his perfect plan to make me perfect. Jesus' heart on the matter was this: "Now my heart is troubled, and what shall I say? 'Father, save me from this hour?' No, it was for this very reason I came to this hour. Father, glorify your name!" (John 12:27).

LIFE APPLICATION

1. When are you tempted to say to God, "This is too hard"?

2. Do you feel "numb" sometimes? Is there some pain you're cushioning yourself against and not allowing yourself to feel? Why are you afraid? How will God help you if you face it?

3. How would a deeper knowledge of God's word produce a deeper security in your relationship with God? What can you do to grow in your knowledge of the Scriptures?

4. What scriptures are you unwilling to fulfill by the way you live your life? What do you learn from Jesus that challenges you to change your unwillingness and to repent?

·30·
Eyes Opened to Faith
Disciples on the Road to Emmaus

JEANIE SHAW
Boston, Massachusetts

Read Luke 24:13-35

> Now that same day two of them were going to a village called Emmaus, about seven miles from Jerusa-lem. They were talking with each other about every-thing that had happened. As they talked and discussed these things with each other, Jesus himself came up and walked along with them; but they were kept from recognizing him.
> "...It is true! The Lord has risen and has appeared to Simon." Then the two told what had happened on the way, and how Jesus was recognized by them when he broke the bread.
> Luke 24:13-16, 34-35

Across an ocean lives a nine-year-old boy who has never known the love of a family. He does not eat balanced meals, has never worn a new piece of clothing and is often cold. He does not yet know it, but he is going to be our son. Here, he will have a room, warm clothes, as well as a mom and dad, two sisters and a brother who all love him and pray for him every day. Hours of paperwork, much prayer and many dollars have been spent on our son. In a few months, when we adopt him, he will leave his country, his friends and his language and step into a plane with two strangers, heading to a place he has never seen that he will soon call home.

How will he be able to do this? Somehow he will have faith that the life planned for him is better than the life he knows now by sight.

Jesus knows the struggle we have to live by faith when we so naturally live by sight. Yet, he wants us to grasp, to truly understand, that what seems is less significant than what is promised. He calls us to deny experience and rely on what is promised, rather than deny his promises and rely on experience. It is a battle he observed from heaven since the beginning. He left the glory of heaven and his Father to come here to show us how to live, to save us and to show us God in the flesh. He never quit loving us or giving to us even while being misunderstood, hated, forgotten and crucified. He never quit teaching us how to live by faith.

Will He Find Faith?

In the first century the world could see Jesus' miracles, hear his amazing teaching and experience the compassion of God in the flesh. Jesus demonstrated faith in his own life. He challenged lack of faith in the disciples. He taught parables about faith. In Luke 18:1-8 Jesus tells a parable to teach the disciples to pray and never give up. He ends the parable with a question: "When the Son of Man comes, will he find faith on the earth?" Jesus longed for this question to be answered with a resounding Yes!

After Jesus had been crucified and resurrected he had completed the path to the Father for us. He could have gone on home to be with his Father. However, he chose to remain here to see his friends again. We learn from the Scripture that he wanted to make sure his disciples realized and believed that he had risen from the dead. He wanted to build their faith so they could pass it on to others.

So, Jesus entered the earth scene again on the road to Emmaus. Not a dramatic entrance—he just joined two disciples as they walked and talked together. He wanted to know their hearts. Where was their faith? How were they responding to what he had taught while he was with them? How disappointing it must have been for Jesus to hear their thoughts. They still didn't get it. He did not find faith on the earth. How could this be? And yet, in Luke 24:27-53 he had the patience once again to teach them about himself, using the Scriptures. He persevered with them. He did not walk away in disgust and give up on them. Verse 28 shows that he waited to see if their faith would revive.

He did not push himself on them as they arrived at the village.

Walking with Jesus

Likewise, we must respond to Jesus' pursuit of us with our pursuit of him. He will not continue to walk alongside someone who does not want him there. For those men, being with Jesus filled a longing in them that nothing else could fill. They strongly urged him to stay with them. When they broke bread with Jesus, it all came together. They had done this before. It really was Jesus! What he said really was true! Now Jesus was ready to leave them and visit with the Eleven (Luke 24:33).

The disciples though, even with the testimony of the women, doubted. Later, even when Jesus stood in front of them, they thought he was a ghost. What hid their understanding? They were inexperienced at living by faith and fearful of it, as well (Luke 9:45). They were troubled and anxious, true signs of faithlessness. Jesus tells them to look, to touch. He even eats real food in their presence. He longs for them to grasp that he is real. Can't you hear him say, "I'm for real, guys. And what I say is really going to happen!"

Jesus was dead, yet he lived again—he was walking, talking, eating. He defied science and human understanding. I think, *How could they be so foolish? How could they be so slow? They had been with him.* But they had also seen him die. Their "sight" and understanding stopped there. It *seemed* that he was dead, yet, the resurrection was real. All his promises and plans were real. Understanding this, they would begin to learn to live each day by faith.

Lest I become self righteous, I must think, *What about me?* Jesus gives me the promise of loving concern and provision, treasures in heaven, fields ripe for harvest, a way out for every temptation, power to change, joy, peace that passes understanding, and on and on. Yet, I can get worried and anxious, caught up in the cares of physical life, discouraged and stuck in a rut at times. It is the same struggle the disciples had 2,000 years ago. But Jesus will walk also with me on that road to Emmaus and break bread with me. He will reveal himself to me more clearly, look in my heart, hear my words to him, so that in me he will find faith on the earth.

LIFE APPLICATION

1. Remember when you first developed the faith that now saves you. How long was your Emmaus road? Who helped you along the way? Are you grateful for Jesus' and others' patience with you?

2. How has your faith grown over time? List some of the big hurdles you have jumped with faith.

3. What is the greatest challenge to your faith at the moment? What steps are you taking to increase your faith and overcome? Who can help you?

· 31 ·
From Doubt to Faith
The Apostle Thomas

CURT SIMMONS
Warsaw, Poland

Read John 20:24-29

> A week later his disciples were in the house again, and Thomas was with them. Though the doors were locked, Jesus came and stood among them and said, "Peace be with you!"
>
> John 20:26

Early on, Jesus had seen something special in Thomas. Among the masses of interested hopefuls anticipating the Messiah's arrival, Thomas had established himself as someone Jesus could use to convince any doubters. But could he be one of the Twelve? Would a three-year training program with Thomas prepare him to be a main mover in the establishment of Jesus' church on earth? Did he have sufficient qualifications among the thousands of candidates to be an apostle? An all-night prayer session had finally convinced Jesus (Luke 6:12-16). Thomas was to be one of the Twelve. He was in, and Jesus would do anything and everything to make sure he would never be out.

Faithful Thomas

The selection was solid. When religious leaders hurled accusations of demon-possession at Jesus and family members spoke boldly of his need for a "psychiatrist," Thomas dismissed the claims, continued to believe and stayed true to his friend (Mark 3:20-30). He had accepted the rigorous schedule of an apostle and the accountability that accompanied it. He had submitted to the high standard of his calling and the infrequent times of rest and relaxation. He had swallowed the many painful doses of discipline prescribed by the Great Physician and accepted regular rebukes for faithlessness, worldliness and selfishness. When called by Jesus to return to Judea where persecution was at its peak, Thomas was eager and willing not only to go with Jesus, but to die with him (John 11:1-16, especially v. 16).

During his three-year relationship with Thomas, Jesus had loved him, trusted him, rebuked him, prayed with him, served with him, taught him, vacationed with him, endured persecution with him, encouraged him and trained him. He was not about to lose him. The one who had taught the masses to leave the ninety-nine and look for the one was now proving he was not a hypocrite (Luke 15:1-7). The man who taught and displayed God's patience with our sins and shortcomings wanted to be with his friend.

Doubtful Thomas

Thomas was not with the Eleven when Jesus first appeared to them. Perhaps he was distraught that his leader and friend was now really gone, and life without him was unthinkable. Whatever caused him to be absent during the Lord's first resurrection appearance to his apostles, Thomas had missed the initial proof-positive presentation of the holes in the hands, feet and side. He hadn't felt the "overjoyed" sensation of seeing the Lord alive again as the other ten had. It was time for Jesus to show these convincing proofs to Thomas, as well. It was time to offer him "peace." It was time for Thomas to stop doubting and believe.

Jesus was not going to stop until Thomas was back, until he had been given an opportunity to put his doubts to death. This event in John 20 is not necessarily a rebuke, but a reminder to one of his best friends that Jesus wanted him enough to come looking for him and would seek until he found.

The "Thomas" in Us

There were times when God revealed a lot of weakness and sin in Patty's and my marriage and in our overall lives. We needed to make some serious changes. It was great to get help, but because of our failings, we doubted God's love. Other challenges came along, and we began to feel useless. We wondered if God even wanted us in his church anymore.

Because of friends who loved us, came looking for us and believed in us, we began to regain our faith and vision. Though the spiritual doors to our hearts were locked, Jesus entered our lives, as he did Thomas' life, saying, "Stop doubting and believe."

Life hasn't been the same since. Yes, there have been trials and ups and downs. But both Patty and I look back to those times as the times when we finally and firmly believed that God loved us, wanted us and was willing to come look for us, even in our sorry condition. Our successes since that time can be directly attributed to the love of God we felt then—the same love seen here in this interaction between Jesus and Thomas.

Stuck in Spiritual Mud

All of us need consistent reminders about who Jesus really is. Maybe you've been faithful to God for years but recently did something you thought you would never do. Now you're afraid to admit it and even more afraid that God won't forgive you or come looking for you. Perhaps it was a sexual sin or a fit of rage. Maybe you cussed at somebody or are trying to cover up for a lie you told. Or maybe you've been working hard for the Lord year after year but, looking back, you can't point to anything significant to prove it was all worth the effort. You're struggling in a big way and perhaps even contemplating quitting.

So what does Jesus think of you now that you're struggling? What does Jesus have in mind to do with you when you doubt, or when you no longer feel like being with other Christians and just want to get away? When you're stuck in spiritual mud, will Jesus come with a rebuke or with a rope to pull you out?

Help arrived for Thomas! Jesus came and stood among them and said, "Peace be with you!" Then he said to Thomas, "Put your finger here; see my hands. Reach out your hand and put it into my side. Stop doubting and believe" (John 20:27).

As Thomas went on to greatness after this encounter with Jesus, so can you. He played a major role in the evangelization of the world in the first century and ended his life in glory as a martyr for Jesus—a fitting response to the man who loved him, looked for him, believed in him and longed to bring him back.

LIFE APPLICATION

1. When do you find yourself doubting God's love for you?

2. Examine the times in your Christian life when you were not doing well and the specific ways you now see how God worked to get you back on track.

3. Why do we have a hard time believing God still wants to pursue a relationship with us even when we're not that strong?

4. What can you do from this point on to prevent these times of doubt in your life?

Still With the People
Epilogue

TOM A. JONES
Hermitage, Tennessee

Jesus, when he came to earth, was almost always with the people. His moments away from others were times to draw strength from his fellowship with God so he could wade back in to those places where the needs were really found. He did not live his life in monastic seclusion. He did not just speak to crowds from a distance. He did not hide behind a wall of lieutenants who did all the dirty work. He did not leave people thinking that he was not quite there with them emotionally. He went where the people were, and he was with them heart and soul.

Those of us who are leaders need to pay special attention. Yes, Jesus had times with leaders and "would-be" leaders, but he lived a lifestyle that was oriented to the common man and woman. The encounters we have considered in this book were the rule in his life, not the exception. Leaders will always need time with other leaders, but if that ever causes us to neglect the people with no positions or no titles, we will have taken a path that leads away from Jesus.

When Jesus left, the people knew they had been with him. They could not forget being with him. For as long as they lived, they remembered being with him, and surely those memories would sometimes comfort them, sometimes challenge them and sometimes haunt them. He left his mark on all who met him.

Some people left Jesus sad, some angry, some totally renewed, but I can't imagine that anyone ever left Jesus thinking that he didn't care. (I probably should take that back since our potential for criticalness and self-pity is almost unlimited.) But the point is that Jesus was always *demonstrating* to someone that he cared for them.

Whether it was one of his Twelve, whom he saw every day (and all through the day), or a strange soul who had never laid eyes on him, he did something in their lives that mattered. Sometimes he touched. Sometimes he healed. Sometimes he gave hope. Sometimes he spoke truth that was hard to hear. Sometimes he wept. But in it all, he defined for us what a human being is supposed to be: one who loves God with all this heart and soul and loves his neighbor as himself.

We started this book with the idea that, for all of us, there is more of Jesus that we don't know than we do know. Having worked for several months with this material, I feel I do know Jesus better, but I also have the conviction that there is so much more of him I want to know.

Just a few days before I wrote this epilogue, I sat on the third row in Madison Square Garden in New York City at a service attended by more than 16,000 souls, most of whom have decided that they too want to know as much about Jesus as they can learn. At one point during the final song (a Zulu tune from South Africa), I turned around and just savored the moment. This huge arena, which has played host to so many famous performers and athletes, was literally rocking to a song about Jesus, a man who lived twenty centuries ago.

I stood in awe. It was the most Christians I had ever seen in one building up to that time. As I looked at the joy on the faces, as I felt the vibrations of celebration, as I watched the clapping hands and swaying bodies in the dim corners of this famous place, I knew that as we enter the twenty-first century, *Jesus is still with the people*. Just how he does it in these days, I don't always know. But as the risen Christ, he is still touching, still healing, still speaking truth and still changing lives.

What will you do with what you have learned here? Will it cause you to be more of a servant, more of a giver, more a person who shows others what sacrificial love looks like? That is the test of the time you have spent with this book. Jesus was able to be this way with the people, because he knew also how to be *with* God. If Jesus' life humbles us, if it causes us to spend more time with God, asking to be like him, and if it leads us give ourselves—heart and soul—to people, our exercise will have changed the world.

The Enduring Impact of Jesus
Appendix

TONEY MULHOLLAN
Spring, Texas

> "But I tell you the truth, it is better for you that I go away. When I go away, I will send the Helper to you.... When the Helper comes, he will prove to the people of the world the truth about sin, about being right with God, and about judgment."
>
> John 16:7–8 NCV

Jesus made it clear to his disciples that his earthly ministry was coming to a close. This transition would not be an ending but would usher in a time when his influence would multiply. With the power of the Holy Spirit (the Helper), the life of Jesus has affected every corner of our globe. More than just being known, his teachings have transformed lives, cultures and nations. There is even now a battle of right and wrong, good and evil, spiritual and unspiritual, and between the godly and ungodly. We can take heart that the Spirit is at work to help us overcome the world. Even a cursory look at the influence of Jesus through history will give us hope for what lies ahead. Let's look at two different aspects of his impact.

The Impact of Jesus on Helping the Poor

Most societies before Christianity were cold and indifferent to the poor. Scholars have exhaustively searched through ancient historical documents, and there is little or no trace of any organized charitable efforts. Before Christ, structured benevolence is largely unknown, but with the spread of Christianity, helping the needy moves to the forefront and flourishes.

Jesus makes a clarion call to help the poor. In the powerful discourse from Jesus in Matthew 25, he says:

> "I was hungry, and you gave me food. I was thirsty, and you gave me something to drink. I was alone and away

from home, and you invited me into your house. I was without clothes, and you gave me something to wear. I was sick, and you cared for me. I was in prison, and you visited me" (Matthew 25:35-36 NCV).

He then goes on to say in verse 40, "I tell you the truth, anything you did for even the least of my people here, you also did for me." Jesus commanded and encouraged generosity and even called some disciples to give all their wealth to the poor.

This generosity was also unique in its purpose. It was not giving just for the sake of meeting needs. Hand-in-hand with this benevolence was the call to accept Christ. As you study the gospels, you can see that Jesus never separated his teaching ministry from his healing ministry. He never healed the sick, fed the poor, or raised the dead without also calling his hearers to embrace a relationship with God. Jesus at one point even rebukes a crowd and says, "I tell you the truth, you aren't looking for me because you saw me do miracles. You are looking for me because you ate the bread and were satisfied" (John 6:26 NCV). It is a natural tendency to subtly shift our emphasis in helping the poor and neglect to call people to make Jesus Lord. Helping the poor is rarely controversial, but the call to follow God is. We do humanity a great disservice when we neglect either aspect of this powerful tandem of outreach to a hurting world.

The Christian call to help the poor is also unique in that it is not just directed inward. True, we are called to meet the needs of believers first. Romans 12:13 in the New Century Version says, "Share with God's people who need help. Bring strangers in need into your homes" and John admonishes in 1 John 3:17, "Suppose someone has enough to live and sees a brother or sister in need, but does not help. Then God's love is not living in that person." Beyond the body of Christ, we are also called to serve the world and even those who oppose us. Jesus said, "If you love only the people who love you, you will get no reward. Even the tax collectors do that. And if you are nice only to your friends, you are no better than other people. Even those who don't know God are nice to their friends" (Matthew 5:46-47 NCV). And lest we miss the point, Jesus makes it exceedingly clear when he says, "But love your enemies, do good to them, and lend to them without hoping to get anything back. Then you will have a great reward, and you will be children of the Most High God..." (Luke 6:35 NCV). This call is unique among world religions: not only to help our own but to love and serve even those who oppose us.

The history of the early church is a rich example of how disciples carried out the teachings of Christ. The book of Acts reflects his spirit as we see the church meeting the needs of one another, churches meeting the needs of sister churches and even Paul taking up collections to serve not only the Jerusalem church but his countrymen as well (Acts 24:17).

Even enemies of the early church marveled at the love of the Christians. The last Roman emperor who tried to destroy the Christian movement, Julian "the Apostate" wrote: "For it is disgraceful that, when no Jew ever has to beg, and the impious Galileans [Christians] support both their own poor and ours as well, all men see that our people lack aid from us." It is a powerful testimony when even your harshest persecutor recognizes your acts of service to the needy.

From the earliest years of the church, through the middle ages, to the present day, the call to help the poor has impacted the world. Even in the last 200 years the largest and most effective organizations for helping the poor have been Christian based in their origins. Most orphanages in eighteenth-century England were run by Christian churches. The YMCA and YWCA were originally founded to meet the physical and spiritual needs of the poor in urban areas. The Salvation Army, which is in scores of countries, has its roots in Christian outreach and meeting physical needs. Thousands of organizations could be named (our own HOPE worldwide is a worthy example) that were or are organized, motivated and moved by the principles that Jesus taught about meeting the needs of the poor.

This legacy attests to the enduring power of Jesus' words. Let's continue to reflect his balance of teaching, serving and meeting the needs of a hurting world. "Then the King will answer, 'I tell you the truth, anything you did for even the least of my people here, you also did for me'" (Matthew 25:40 NCV).

The Impact of Jesus on Learning and Education

First and foremost, Jesus knew the Word. His most ardent critics observed it: "The Jews there were amazed and asked, 'How did this man get such learning without having been taught?'" (John 7:15). Even guards who were sent to arrest Jesus exclaimed, "No one ever spoke the way this man does" (John 7:46). He knew the Word so well that his teaching stood out from his contemporaries: "When Jesus had finished saying these things, the crowds were amazed at his teaching, because he taught as one who had authority, and not as their teachers of the law" (Matthew 7:28–29). His critics constantly attempted to trip him up or challenge his grasp on the word of God. Luke 11:53–54 says, "When Jesus went outside, the Pharisees and the teachers of the law began to oppose him fiercely and to besiege him with questions, waiting to catch him in something he might say." They were unsuccessful in all their attempts. Jesus not only knew the Word but even challenged his critics: "Are you not in error because you do not know the Scriptures or the power of God?" (Mark 12:24). He answered all questions and challenges to his ministry and knowledge of the Word so well that Mark 12:34 records, "And from then on no one dared ask him any more questions." That is knowing the Word!

Jesus not only knew the Word but called all his disciples to know it as well. He said,

> "If anyone hears my words but does not keep them, I do not judge that person. For I did not come to judge the world, but to save the world. There is a judge for the one who rejects me and does not accept my words; the very words I have spoken will condemn them at the last day. For I did not speak on my own, but the Father who sent me commanded me to say all that I have spoken. I know that his command leads to eternal life. So whatever I say is just what the Father has told me to say" (John 12:47–50).

The understanding that we will be judged by the words of God and his Son, Jesus, has been a great impetus for disciples to be learners. It is imperative that we grasp the Word, understand it and live it. Early disciples demonstrated this kind of commitment to knowing the Word. Even the very first sermon preached by Peter on the day of Pentecost is full of direct quotes from the from the Old Testament. In fact, New Testament writers quote the Old Testament well over 260 times. This shows their knowledge of the Scripture (understanding that the Old Testament was the only Scripture that early Christians had, as the New Testament was only beginning to be written). As disciples today, it also shows the importance of knowing the Old Testament Scriptures as well as we know the New. A thorough knowledge of both is key. Bible teacher John Oakes points this out in his book, *From Shadow to Reality*: "So many of the teachings and even the events in the Old Testament only make sense when they find themselves fulfilled in the pages of the New Testament."

Early Christian writers were prolific in their knowledge and quoting of Scripture. David Dalrymple, who wrote three volumes on early Christian history, said,

> As I possessed all the existing works of the Fathers of the second and third centuries, I commenced to search, and up to this time I have found the entire New Testament, except eleven verses.

That is amazing—if all Bibles were confiscated we would still be able to reassemble the Bible from just the quotations that early Christians included in their writings and letters.

Christians have often been called the "people of the book." It implies a literate people. This teaching concept flows from the earliest part of Scripture. Deuteronomy 6:6–7 says,

> These commandments that I give you today are to be on your hearts. Impress them on your children. Talk about them when you sit at home and when you walk along the road, when you lie down and when you get up.

The Christian religion is a teaching religion. As the Christian faith has spread, so has education. Even during the "dark ages" it was Christian priests and monks who kept learning alive by hand-copying Scripture and great literary works of the past.

The invention of the printing press was a vital factor in getting God's word into the hands of the masses, as it gave birth to the Gutenberg Bible. Johann Gutenberg (AD 1398–1468) was not the first to invent the printing press, but he was the first to develop the methods that made mass production possible. Gutenberg said, "I know what I want to do: I wish to print the Bible." It was this mass production of the Bible that eventually led to the Reformation and Restoration Movements of the last several centuries.

The Christian emphasis on learning played a key role in the formation of many of our institutions of higher learning. Of the first 108 colleges in America, 106 were begun by believers. By the close of the year 1860, there were 246 colleges in America. Seventeen were state institutions; the rest were founded by Christian groups or by individuals with an avowed Christian purpose. It is interesting to note that in 1777, the Continental Congress voted to spend $300,000 to purchase Bibles to be distributed throughout the thirteen colonies, to be used in schools! In America there are over 1000 colleges with Christian affiliation.

Christian education has not only influenced America, it has also influenced many third world countries. Countless Christian missionaries have educated people in the remotest of jungles, in the poorest of countries and among the most illiterate of peoples. In fact, a great number of the world's languages were first set to writing by Christian missionaries so that people could read God's word in their own language. Wycliffe Bible Translators has been at the forefront of this work and is still laboring to reach 160 million people who do not have the Bible in their language.

The influence of Jesus on education and learning has been immeasurable. Our first priority as Christians is to know the Word ourselves, and then to teach it to as many people as we can. Let's help fulfill the prophecy of Jeremiah:

> "No longer will they teach their neighbor,
> or say to one another, 'Know the LORD,'
> because they will all know me,
> from the least of them to the greatest,"
> declares the LORD (Jeremiah 31:34).

www.ipibooks.com